The Book of
PRESENTS

The Book of PRESENTS

edited by Sonya Mills

Contents

easy to make gifts for every occasion

Pantheon Books
New York

CONTRIBUTORS

Carpentry
Jeanne Argent; Stuart Dalby; *Pins and Needles*;
Ernest Roth
Cookery
Cammerloher Kitchens; Margery Lodge;
Sonya Mills
Crafts
Jeanne Argent; Kate Bonella; David Constable of
Candlemakers Supplies, Helen Donnellan;
Anne Filbey: Ruth Francis; Chris Grundy;
Valerie Janitch; *Living*; Diana Mansour;
Kit Pyman; Janet Wedgewood
Crochet, Knitting and Sewing
Lisa Pryde; *Living*
Presenting Your Presents
Sara Cole
Small Presents
Nicola Chambers; Hilary More; Barbara
Pickering; Gillian Roth

The publishers would also like to thank the
following for their assistance in preparing this
book:
Candlemakers Supplies; DRG Sellotape
Products; Dylon International Ltd; Paperchase
Products Ltd.

Photography by Peter Howard Smith except
John Morfett pp 31, 35; *Living* pp 29, 57, 63, 65;
Bill McLaughlin pp 50; *Pins and Needles* pp 127.

Diagrams by Hayward Art Group

List of mail order suppliers

J. C. Penney Inc.
1301 Ave. of the Americas
New York, NY 10019

Sears, Roebuck & Co.
Dept 139 CHC
4640 Roosevelt Blvd
Philadelphia, Pa 19132

Montgomery Ward
Dept CHC
Montgomery Ward Plaza
Chicago, Ill 60681

American Handicrafts
508 Sixth Avenue
New York, NY 10011

Economy Handicrafts
50-21 69th Street
Woodside, NY 11377

Originally published in the United Kingdom
by London Editions Ltd/W. H. Smith &
Son Ltd.

Library of Congress Cataloging in Publication
Data

Mills, Sonya, 1936–
  The book of presents.

  Includes index.
  1. Handicraft.   2. Cookery.   3. Gifts.   I. Title.
TT157.M493   745.5   79-2187
ISBN 0-394-50782-7

Designed and produced in the United
Kingdom by London Editions Limited

Printed in the United Kingdom by Severn
Valley Press Limited

First American Edition

Giving presents is fun – almost as much fun as receiving them – particularly if you have made them yourself. And, quite apart from the satisfaction of making beautiful gifts, you save money.

The hard part is deciding what to make and how to set about it so that the result is as good as or better than anything available in the shops. So I have tried to include in this book a treasure trove of presents to make for all your friends and for every member of the family, from the very youngest to the oldest – there's even something for the cat and the dog.

The presents cover a wide range of skills and crafts – sewing, cookery, crochet, plastic casting, knitting, leatherwork, candlemaking and many others – and there is almost certainly at least one skill you have already set your hand to. But try some of the others – though the presents may all look highly professional and impressive, most of them are straightforward and simple to make. The secret lies in their good, imaginative design and in the care you take over the finishing. So you might just as well surprise yourself and try something completely new.

There are plenty of things for children, including wooden toys, knitted toys and clothes, because they especially love having things made for them. Something made by a parent will be treasured long after a shop-bought article has been smashed or lost. There are also plenty of presents which are simple enough for children to make, so the whole family can set out on a creative spree.

If you have decided that this time you are going to make all your Christmas gifts, it is no good trying to tackle something that will eat up every leisure moment for the next eighteen months. The more ambitious items in this book may need a little more of your time than some of the others, but even the most complicated will not take an inordinate amount of time and the majority of the presents can be made very quickly.

Our designs are only starting points, and you can develop and adapt them to suit your friends. Even a change of colour can make an enormous difference – for example our family sweaters could equally well be knitted in constrasting electric colours, or you could give the corner shelf an antique finish.

Cost is an important factor – I have tried with the designers to make things as economically as possible. If you think that something, such as the brandied fruit, is expensive, a look at shop prices will soon change your mind. Most of the presents are very cheap to make and don't require expensive equipment.

Before buying your materials, have a look at the chapter 'Getting the Professional Look', which give hints on avoiding waste as well as on how to reach a first-class standard.

I hope you enjoy browsing through this book and choosing your presents. A very happy Christmas/Birthday/House-warming to you, your family and all your friends!

Sonya Mills

Crochet

Versatile Shawl

A traditional garment which has made a big come-back, a shawl has many uses. This lacy crocheted one is perfect for wearing over a bare-arm evening dress, and also comes in handy to throw over a summer frock on a chilly evening, or for reading in bed. Its soft magnolia shade will go with almost any color.

Materials
350g [12oz] 4-ply fingering yarn
Size H crochet hook

Size
Length at center back 114cm [45in]
Across top edge 160cm [63in]

Gauge
1 pattern = 6cm [2⅜in] wide
4 rows = 5cm [2in] deep

Start at center back neck. Make 6 ch, 3 dc into 4th ch from hook, 1 ch, (3 dc 1 ch 3 dc) into next ch. 1 ch, 4 dc into last ch.
1st row 3 ch for 1st dc, 3 dc between 1st and 2nd dc, 3 ch, 2 dc in sp, 3 ch, (3 dc 1 ch 3 dc) in next sp, 3 ch, 2 dc in next sp, 3 ch, 4 dc between last 2 dcs.
2nd row 3 ch, 3 dc between 1st and 2nd dc, 3 ch, 2 dc in dcs, 3 ch, 2 dc in ch sp, 3 ch, (3 dc 1 ch 3 dc) in center sp, 3 ch, 2 dc in ch sp, 3 ch, 2 dc in dcs, 3 ch, 4 dc between last 2 dcs.
3rd row 3 ch, 3 dc between 1st and 2nd dc, 3 ch, 2 dc, 3 ch, (2 dc 1 ch 2 dc) between next 2 dcs, 3 ch, (3 dc 1 ch 3 dc) in center sp, 3 ch, (2 dc 1 ch 2 dc) between next 2 dcs, 3 ch, 2 dc, 3 ch, 4 dc between last 2 dcs.
4th row 3 ch, 3 dc between 1st and 2nd dc, 3 ch, 2 dc, 3 ch, (2 dc 1 ch 2 dc) in ch sp, 3 ch, 2 dc in ch sp, 3 ch, (3 dc 1 ch 3 dc) in center sp, 3 ch, 2 dc in ch sp, 3 ch, (2 dc 1 ch 2 dc) in ch sp, 3 ch, 2 dc, 3 ch, 4 dc between last 2 dcs.
5th row 3 ch, 3 dc, 3 ch, 2 dc, 3 ch, (2 dc 1 ch 2 dc), 3 ch, 2 dc, 3 ch, 2 dc in ch sp, 3 ch, (3 dc 1 ch 3 dc), 3 ch, 2 dc in ch sp, 3 ch, 2 dc, 3 ch, (2 dc 1 ch 2 dc), 3 ch, 2 dc, 3 ch, 4 dc between last 2 dcs.
6th row 3 ch, 3 dc, 3 ch, 2 dc, 3 ch, (2 dc 1 ch 2 dc), 3 ch, 2 dc, 3 ch, (2 dc 1 ch 2 dc) between next 2 dcs, 3 ch, (3 dc 1 ch 3 dc), 3 ch, (2 dc 1 ch 2 dc) between next 2 dcs, 3 ch, 2 dc, 3 ch (2 dc 1 ch 2 dc), 3 ch, 2 dc, 3 ch, 4 dc between last 2 dcs.

Rows 4–6 inclusive form pat. Rep, taking extra sts into pat as they form, until 53 rows including foundation row are completed, ending with a 4th pat row. Fasten off.

Fringe
Cut remaining yarn into 50cm [20in] lengths. Knot 6 strands in end of each pat (in 1 ch sp and between 2 dcs) along side edges of shawl. Divide each knot in half and knot across as shown in picture.

Abbreviations

beg	beginning
ch	chain
dc	double crochet
dec	decrease
dtr	double treble
hdc	half double crochet
inc	increase
pat	pattern
rep	repeat
rnd	round
sc	single crochet
sk	skip
sl st	slip stitch
sp(s)	space(s)
tog	together
tr	treble crochet

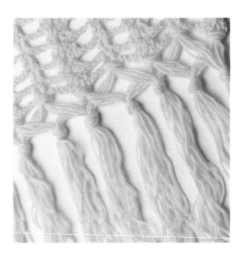

Fluffy Bedjacket

Crocheted in soft mohair yarn, this lacy bedjacket feels as soft and warm as it looks.

Materials
350g [12oz] medium weight mohair yarn
Size F and G crochet hooks
Five buttons

Size
To fit 91–102cm [36–40in] bust loosely
Length 57cm [22½in]
Sleeve length 43cm [17in]

Gauge
13 dc × 6 rows = 7.5cm [3in] with size F hook and double crochets

Abbreviations
1 dc f (1 double crochet forward): insert hook around front of st to give raised dc (keep dc at front of work on every row)

Yoke
With size F hook and starting at neck edge make 67 ch.
Foundation row 1 dc in 4th ch from hook; 1 dc in each ch to end = 65 sts.
1st row 3 ch for 1st dc * 1 dc f, 1 dc; rep from * to end.
2nd row 3 ch, 1 dc in base of ch, * 1 dc f, 2 dc in dc; rep from * to end = 98 sts.
3rd and 4th rows 3 ch, 1 dc * 1 dc f, 2 dc; rep from * to end.
5th row 3 ch, 2 dc in dc * 1 dc f, 2 dc in dc, 1 dc; rep from * to end = 131 sts.
6th and 7th rows 3 ch, 2 dc * 1 dc f, 3 dc; rep from * to end.
8th row 3 ch, 2 dc in dc, 1 dc * 1 dc f, 1 dc, 2 dc in dc, 1 dc; rep from * to end = 164 sts.
Inc 1 dc in center of dc panel on every 3rd row twice more = 230 sts. Work 3 more rows. Change to size G hook and divide for back and fronts.
Next row 35 sc, make 12 ch, sk 45 dc, 70 sc, make 12 ch, sk 45 dc, 35 sc.
Next row 1 ch, 1 sc * 3 ch, sk 2 sts, 1 sc in next st; rep from * 25 times. Working along ch loops at armhole (3 ch, sk 1 st, 1 sc in next st) twice, 3 ch, sk 2 sts, 1 sc in next st (3 ch, sk 1 st, 1 sc in next st) twice * 3 ch, sk 2 sts, 1 sc in next st; rep from * to last st, 1 sc = 55 loops.

Main pattern : 1st row 3 ch, 1 dc in sc
* 3 ch, 1 sc in loop, 3 ch, 3 dc in next
loop; rep from * to last loop, 3 ch, 1 sc
in loop, 3 ch, 2 dc in last st.
2nd row 3 ch, 1 sc in 1st loop * 3 ch,
1 sc in next loop; rep from * to last
loop, 1 ch, 1 hdc in last st.
3rd row 4 ch * 3 dc in loop, 3 ch, 1 sc
in next loop, 3 ch; rep from * to last
loop; 3 dc, 2 ch, 1 hdc in last st.
4th row 1 ch, 1 sc in loop * 3 ch, 1 sc
in next loop; rep from * to last loop;
1 sc in 2nd ch.
These 4 rows form pat : rep 5 times
more, then 1st and 2nd rows. Fasten off.

Sleeves

Starting at center of underarm ch, pick
up 21 3 ch loops around armhole and
work in pat as for back until sleeve
measures 40.5cm [16in] ending with a
3rd pat row.
Cuff With size F hook, work 1 sc in
1st st * 1 sc in loop, 1 sc in center dc,
1 sc in next loop, rep 10 times from *,
1 sc in 3rd ch = 35 sts. Work in holes for
6 rows.
Picot edge 2 sc * 5 ch, sl st into 4th ch
from hook, 1 ch, sk 1 hdc, 1 sc in each
of next 2 sts; rep from * to end. Fasten
off.

Neck

With size F hook work 4 rows in
hdcs. Work picot edging, fasten off.

Front Edging

Work 1 row sc along front yoke edges,
making 2 ch loops on right side for
buttonholes.

Finishing

Sew sleeve seams and sew on buttons.

Afghan and Matching Pillow

A very special present: an afghan lap rug and matching pillow, luxuriously fringed, in rich glowing colors. Perfect for snuggling into on cold nights, or to use in the car or on picnics. They are quite simple to make – basic crochet bands are interwoven with yarn in the same color sequence.

Afghan

Materials
Knitting worsted yarn:
1,250g [45oz] in wine
300g [11oz] in orange
200g [8oz] in fawn
100g [4oz] in blue and red
Size I crochet hook
Large yarn needle

Size
122 × 165cm [48 × 65in] excluding fringe

Gauge
14 sts (7 dc) × 7½ rows = 10cm [4in]
Note When working dcs insert hook under 3 threads of previous row to ensure a firm fabric.

Use yarn double throughout. With size I hook and wine make 185 ch.
Foundation row 1 dc into 5th ch from hook * 1 ch, sk 1 ch, 1 dc in next ch; rep from * to end = 91 sps.
Pat row 3 ch, sk 1st dc, 1 dc in next dc * 1 ch, 1 dc in next dc; rep from * to end working last dc in 2nd of turning ch.
Rep pat row throughout, working in color sequence of 4 rows wine, 2 orange, 1 fawn, 3 wine, 1 blue, 4 wine, 1 orange, 2 wine, 1 fawn, 1 red = 20 rows.
Rep 20-row pat 6 times in all, then work 4 rows in wine. Fasten off.

Finishing
Cut yarn into lengths of about 2m [78in] and using 4 strands together weave pat in same color sequence as for crochet.

Fringe
Cut remaining yarn into 30cm [12in] lengths and knot 4 strands through each row end, taking weaving yarn through knot before tightening. Trim fringe.

Beehive Tea Cozy

This delightful crochet tea cozy is made in the shape of an old-fashioned beehive, complete with embroidered honey bees.

Materials
Knitting worsted yarn:
50g [2oz] in light color
50g [2oz] in dark color
Scraps in brown, green, black, yellow
Size H crochet hook

Size
To fit a medium-sized tea pot

Walls (make two)
With light color used double make 32 ch.
Foundation row 1 sc into 4th ch from hook * 1 dc, 1 sc; rep from * to end.
Pattern row 3 ch for 1st dc, * 1 sc into dc, 1 dc into sc; rep from * to last st, 1 sc in top of ch. Rep last row until work measures 10cm [4in]. Fasten off.

Roof
With dark color used double make 5 ch and join into ring, 3 ch for 1st dc, 19 dc into ring, sl st into top of ch.
1st rnd 2 ch working into back loop of sts only, work 1 hdc in each dc, join with sl st.
2nd rnd 2 ch * 2 hdc in back of next st, 1 hdc in back of next st; rep from * to last st, 2 hdc in back of st, join with sl st. Rep 1 st and 2nd rnds twice more, then 1 st rnd twice. Fasten off.

Finishing
Join ends of walls leaving about 6cm [2½in] open in center of seams for spout and handle. On wrong side, hem wall to underside of roof, leaving last row of roof overhanging for eaves. Embroider door on one side in chain stitch. Embroider grass with straight stitches. Make a bee on wall and roof in black and yellow satin stitch, with wings in straight stitch.

Pillow

Materials
Knitting worsted yarn:
225g [8 oz] in wine
50g [2oz] in orange
25g [1oz] in blue, fawn and red
Size F crochet hook
Large yarn needle

Size
33 × 48cm [13 × 19in] excluding fringe

Gauge
16 sts (8 dc) × 9 rows = 7.5cm [3in]
Note When working dcs insert hook
under 3 threads of previous row to
ensure a firm fabric.

With size F hook and wine make 153 ch.
Foundation row 1 dc into 5th ch from
hook * 1 ch, sk 1 ch, 1 dc in next ch;
rep from * to end = 75 sps.
Pat row 3 ch, sk 1st dc, 1 dc in next
dc * 1 ch, 1 dc in next dc; rep from
* to end working last dc in 2nd of
turning ch.
Rep pat row throughout in same color
sequence as for afghan = 20 rows.
Work color pat twice, then work first
15 rows again = 55 rows. Fasten off.

Finishing
Fold pillow in half and join short ends.
With 2 strands of yarn in needle, weave
pat in color sequence as for crochet,
leaving ends of weaving threads loose
at each end of pillow. Knot ends
together and trim fringe to 7.5cm [3in].
Insert foam rubber pad and close
seam.

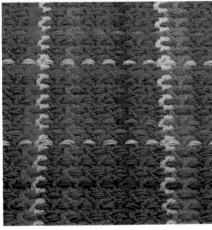

Crochet Vest

Armhole Edging
Starting at center of square at armhole, work 5 rnds in sc around armhole, dec 1 st on every rnd at each corner at base of armhole. Fasten off.

Border
Starting at center lower back, work 5 rnds in sc all around vest; inc 1 st on every rnd at bottom and top corner of fronts, and dec 1 st every rnd at corner of neck. Fasten off.

Fifty-two squares and a crochet edging are all it takes to make this pretty vest. We chose two tones of yellow but there's no end to the color combinations you could choose.

Materials
Knitting worsted yarn:
175g [7oz] in main color
125g [5oz] in contrast color
Size F crochet hook

Size
To fit 89cm [35in] bust
Length 50cm [20in]

Gauge
Each square measures 8.25cm [3¼in]

To make 1 square, with contrast color make 4 ch and join into ring.
1st row 5 ch * 1 dc, 3 ch into ring; rep from * 4 times more; sl st into 3rd of 5 ch.
2nd row 3 ch * 5 dc in 3 ch loop, 1 dc in dc; rep from * 4 times more, 5 dc, sl st into top of 3 ch.
3rd row Break off contrast color; join in main color. 4 ch, 2 dtr in base of ch, 3 ch, 3 dtr in next dc * sk 3 dc, 1 dc, 3ch, 1 dc in next dc, sk 3 dc, 3 dtr in next dc, 3 ch, 3 dtr in next dc. Rep from * twice more, sk 3 dc, 1 dc, 3 ch, 1 dc in next dc, sk 3 dc, sl st into top of 3 ch. Fasten off.
Make 52 squares; sew together as shown in diagram.

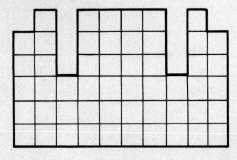

1 square = 1 crochet square

14

Toddler's Coat

Whatever the weather any youngster will be warm as toast in this scarlet coat teamed with frosty white hat and mittens (see page 116).

Materials

550(600:650)g [22(24:26)oz] bulky yarn
Eight buttons (ten for 53cm [21in] length)
4.5mm crochet hook

Size

To fit 53(58:63)cm chest [21(23:25)in]
Actual size 58(63:68)cm [23(25:27)in]
Length 46(48:53)cm [18(19:21)in]
Sleeve with cuff turned back
20(22.5:27)cm [8(9:10½)in]

Gauge

14 sts × 11 rows = 10cm [4in] over pat

Back

With 4.5mm hook make 45(49:53) ch.
Foundation row 1 dc into 3rd ch from hook (1 tr in next ch) twice, * (1 dc in next ch) twice, (1 tr in next ch) twice; rep from * to end.
1st row 1 ch for 1st dc, 1 dc in tr, (1 tr in dc) twice, * (1 dc in tr) twice, (1 tr in dc) twice; rep from * to end.
Cont in pat, working 2 tr over 2 dc and 2 dc over 2 tr. Dec 1 st at each end of 11th and foll 10th row = 40(44:48) sts. Work straight until back measures 28(30.5:35.5cm) [11:12:14in].
Shape armhole * Sl st across 1(2:3) sts, pat to last 1(2:3) sts, turn. Dec 1 st at each end of next 2 rows. Work 1 row. * Rep last 3 rows 3 times more. Then dec 1 st each end of every row until 10(12:14) sts remain. End off.

Sleeves

With 4.5mm hook make 27(29:31) ch.
Work in pat as for back until sleeve measures 15cm [6in]. Inc 1 st each end of next and foll 6th row = 30(32:34) sts. Work straight until sleeve measures

15

sleeve measures 26.5(29:33)cm [10½(11½:13)in]. This allows 5cm [2in] for cuff.
Shape armhole as for back from * to *. Rep last 3 rows until 4 sts remain. Fasten off.

Left Front

Make 31(33:35) ch. Work in pat as for back for 8(10:14) rows. Dec 1 st at beg of next and following 10th row = 28(30:32) sts.
Make buttonhole With wrong side facing pat 2, 2 ch, sk 2 sts, pat to end. Continue straight until front matches back to armhole, making buttonholes on every 8th row. End at side edge. Sl st across 1(2:3) sts, pat to end. Dec 1 st at raglan edge on next 2 rows. Work 1 row. Rep last 3 rows 3 times more, making buttonholes as before. Dec 1 st at armhole edge on every row until 18(19:20) sts remain ending at raglan edge. Dec 1, pat 5(6:7), dec 1, turn. Work 3 rows, then dec 1 st at armhole and 2 sts at neck edge. Fasten off.

Right Front

As left front. The work is reversible.

Collar

Make 39(39:43) ch. Work in pat as for back for 9 rows. Fasten off.

Finishing

Join raglan seams. Join sleeve and side seams. Sew collar to neck, leaving 6 sts at front edge of neck free for overlap. Sew on buttons.

Baby's Cardigan

A useful addition to any young baby's wardrobe, this white crochet cardigan is enlivened with brightly colored embroidery. It will fit a baby up to 6–9 months old.

Materials

80(100)g [3(4)oz] 4-ply baby fingering yarn
Five buttons
Scraps of blue and red embroidery cotton
Size F crochet hook

Sizes

Actual size 46(49.5)cm [18(19½)in] chest
Length 20(23)cm [8(9)in]
Sleeve 14(15)cm [5½(6)in]

Gauge

5½ dc × 3 rows — 2.5cm [1in]

Back and Fronts (all in one)

Make 102(110) ch. 1 sc into 2nd st from hook, 1 sc in each ch to end = 101(109) sts. Work 3 more rows in sc. Begin pattern.
1st row 3 ch * 1 dc in next st, sk next st, 1 ch; rep from * to last 2 sts, 2 dc.
2nd row 3 ch, 1 dc * 1 ch, sk sp (1 dc in next dc, 1 dc in sp) 3 times, 1 dc in dc; rep from * 11(12) times more. 1 ch, sk sp, 2 dc.
3rd row 3 ch, 1 dc * 1 ch, sk sp, 1 dc in next 7 dc; rep from * 11(12) times, 1 ch, sk sp, 2 dc.
4th row as 3rd.
5th row as 1st.
Rows 2–5 inclusive form pat.
Continue working 1 block of pat on fronts and work remainder of body in dcs until work measures 10(12)cm [4(4¾)in].
Divide for armholes Pat 16(17) sts, dc 2 tog, 1 dc, turn. Maintaining pat dec 1 dc at armhole edge on every row until 10(11) sts remain ending at armhole edge (neck edge for larger size).
1st size only: Next row 3 ch, dc 2 tog, dc 2 tog, 1 dc, turn.
Next row 3 ch, dc 2 tog, 1 dc.
Next row 3 ch, dc 2 tog. Fasten off.
2nd size only Sl st across 5 sts; complete as for small size.

Back

Sk 12(13) sts at armhole, join yarn to next st.
1st row 3 ch, dc 2 tog, dc 33(37), dc 2 tog, dc 1, turn.
Continue dec 2 sts on every row until 15(19) sts remain. Fasten off.

Left Front Sk 12(13) sts at armhole, join yarn to next st.
1st row 3 ch, dc 2 tog, pat to end = 18(19) sts. Complete as for other front, reversing shaping.

Sleeves

Make 29(31) ch, 1 sc in 2nd ch from hook, 1 sc to end = 28(30)sc. Work 3 more rows in sc.
Now work in dcs; inc 1 dc each end of next and every 3rd row to 38(40) dcs. Continue straight until sleeve measures 14(15)cm [5½(6)in].
Shape top Sl st across 6 sts, 3 ch, dc 2 tog, dc 20(22), dc 2 tog, 1 dc, turn. Work 1 row.
Next row 3 ch, dc 2 tog, dc 18(20), dc 2 tog, dc 1. Work 1 row.
Now dec 1 dc each end of every row until 6(6) dc remain. Fasten off.

Border

Sew sleeves into raglan armholes. Starting at lower edge of right front work in sc around front and neck edges. Work 5 rows in all, making 5 buttonholes evenly spaced on 3rd row on right front. Fasten off.

Finishing

Embroider each square alternately with red and blue flowers in lazy daisy st.

Cakes and Biscuits

STOLLEN

A traditional Christmas gift in Germany, stollen is yeast bread packed with fruit and nuts. It keeps fresh for several weeks and is best eaten thickly spread with unsalted butter. This recipe makes two medium-sized loaves.

Ingredients
Metric/Imperial
150ml [¼ pint] milk
4 rounded teaspoons dried yeast
100g [4oz] granulated sugar
2 eggs
200g [7oz] butter or margarine
560g [20oz] plain flour
40g [1½oz] chopped mixed peel
40g [1½oz] chopped hazel-nuts
75g [3oz] sultanas
75g [3oz] raisins
50g [2oz] currants
Melted butter
Icing sugar

American
⅝ cup milk
4 rounded teaspoons active dry yeast
½ cup sugar
2 eggs
⅞ cup butter or margarine
5 cups all-purpose flour
¼ cup chopped candied fruits
¼ cup chopped filberts
½ cup light seeded raisins
½ cup dark seedless raisins
⅓ cup dried currants
Melted butter
Confectioners' sugar

Heat the milk until lukewarm; add one teaspoon of the sugar and pour over the yeast. Beat together and let stand in a warm place until frothy.

Put the sugar, eggs and butter in a mixing bowl and leave in a warm place for about twenty minutes, until they can be beaten into a fairly even mixture.

Place the flour in a large warmed mixing bowl. Make a hollow in the middle and pour in the yeast mixture. Stir a little of the flour into this, then cover lightly with flour; do not stir. Leave covered with a cloth until the yeast is bubbling through the flour. Mix together and blend in the egg, sugar and butter mixture. As soon as the mixture starts to blend and set, the fruits and nuts can be gradually kneaded into it.

Turn on to a floured board and knead for at least ten minutes until the dough becomes evenly smooth and loses all stickiness. Return to the bowl, cover with a cloth and put in a warm, but not hot, place. After about ninety minutes the dough should have at least doubled in volume.

Turn out and knead again for about five minutes to remove the larger bubbles. Then return to the warm place to set again for about two hours.

When well risen, turn out on to a floured board and, handling gently, form into a well-rounded oval. Take a rolling pin and press out the half farthest away from you until it is large enough to flap back over the unpressed half (this gives the traditional shape – see picture).

Place on a well-greased baking sheet and let stand again for fifteen minutes. Meanwhile heat the oven to 220°C [425°F, Gas 7]. Bake on center rack for ten minutes, then reduce heat to 200°C [400°F, Gas 6] and bake for thirty minutes more.

Cool on a wire rack. When quite cold, brush with melted butter and dust thickly with sugar.

OLD ENGLISH RUM AND RAISIN CAKE

Full of fruit and redolent of rum this lavish cake makes an impressive gift – preferably to people you're staying with so you get to taste it! Make it well in advance as it needs three weeks to mature, and if you prefer use a medium sweet sherry instead of rum.

Ingredients
Metric/Imperial
175g [6oz] raisins
175g [6oz] currants
225g [8oz] dates
400ml [14fl oz] dark rum or sherry
350g [12oz] plain flour
1 level teaspoon each bicarbonate of soda and baking powder
1 level teaspoon each mixed spice and ground cinnamon
½ level teaspoon grated nutmeg
225g [8oz] butter
225g [8oz] castor sugar
5 eggs

American
1 cup raisins
1 cup dried currants
1⅓ cups pitted dates
1¾ cups dark rum or sherry
3 cups all-purpose flour
1 level teaspoon each baking soda and baking powder
1 level teaspoon each mixed spices and ground cinnamon
½ level teaspoon grated nutmeg
1 cup butter
1 cup finely granulated sugar
5 eggs

Put the fruit in a mixing bowl; pour rum over it, and leave for at least twenty-four hours, preferably 2–3 days, stirring occasionally.

Line a 20cm [8in] round cake pan with greased waxed (greaseproof) paper. Preheat the oven to 150°C [300°F, Gas 2].

Sift the flour, soda, baking powder and spices into a bowl. In another larger bowl cream the butter with the sugar until white and fluffy. Beat in the eggs, one at a time, making sure each one is well mixed in before adding the next. Fold in half the flour mixture, then stir in all the fruit. Fold in remaining flour and combine thoroughly.

The mixture should drop easily from a spoon when tapped; adjust if necessary with more flour or a little milk. Spoon into the prepared pan and bake in the center of the oven for 2–2½ hours, until a cocktail stick set into the middle comes out clean.

Leave in the pan for fifteen minutes, then turn out on to a wire rack to cool. Wrap in foil and store for three weeks.

RICH NUT COOKIES

These super-rich iced cookies make a delicious Christmas treat, and very acceptable small gifts for friends and relations. This recipe makes about eighty.

Ingredients
Metric/Imperial
225g [8oz] margarine or butter
225g [8oz] plain flour
225g [8oz] granulated sugar
225g [8oz] ground hazel-nuts
1 level teaspoon cinnamon
4 egg yolks
100g [4oz] icing sugar
Juice of 1 lemon

American
1 cup margarine or butter
2 cups all-purpose flour
1 cup sugar
1⅓ cups ground filberts
1 level teaspoon cinnamon
4 egg yolks
1 cup confectioners' sugar
Juice of 1 lemon

Blend the butter into the flour until the mixture resembles coarse breadcrumbs. Mix in the sugar, nuts and cinnamon. Stir in the egg yolks to make a firm dough. Refrigerate for thirty minutes.

Preheat the oven to 180°C [350°F, Gas 4].

Roll the dough out on a well-floured board to a good 3mm [⅛in] thick and cut into shapes – traditionally hearts, stars, suns and crescent moons. Place on well-greased baking sheets and bake for about twenty minutes until golden brown. Cool on a wire rack.

Stir enough lemon juice into the sugar to make a stiff icing and spread thinly over the cookies. Leave to harden.

PFEFFERNÜSSE

These traditional hard, German cookies are easy to make, and much spicier than the ones you can buy. This recipe makes about sixty.

Ingredients
Metric/Imperial
250g [9oz] self-raising flour
150g [5oz] granulated sugar
¼ teaspoon each ground ginger, pepper, cloves and cardamom
1 level teaspoon ground cinnamon
1 egg
Milk
100g [4oz] icing sugar

American
2¼ cups self-rising flour
⅝ cup sugar
¼ teaspoon each ground ginger, pepper, cloves and cardamom
1 level teaspoon ground cinnamon
1 egg
Milk
1 cup confectioners' sugar

Sift the flour into a bowl with the sugar and spices. Make a well in the center and break in the egg. Mix together with a knife, slowly adding just enough

milk to make a stiff dough. Refrigerate for thirty minutes.

Preheat the oven to 180°C [350°F, Gas 4].

Roll the dough out thickly – about 1cm [½in] – on a well-floured board, then cut into small circles with a plain cookie cutter or liqueur glass. Place on greased baking sheets, well spaced out, and bake for fifteen minutes. Remove immediately and cool on a wire rack.

Mix the sugar with just enough water to make a stiff icing and brush over each cookie. Leave to harden.

GINGERBREAD MEN

Jolly gingerbread men are fun to make, and children adore them. This recipe makes about ten.

Ingredients
Metric/Imperial
75g [3oz] margarine
2 rounded tablespoons black treacle
50g [2oz] granulated sugar
200g [7oz] plain flour
2 level teaspoons ground ginger
1 level teaspoon mixed spice
½ level teaspoon baking soda

American
3 tablespoons margarine
2 rounded tablespoons molasses
¼ cup sugar
1¾ cups all-purpose flour
2 level teaspoons ground ginger
1 level teaspoon mixed spice
½ level teaspoon baking soda

Heat margarine, molasses (treacle) and sugar together in a small saucepan without boiling. Sift the flour and spices into a bowl.

Dissolve the baking soda in a little water and add to the ingredients in the pan: it will make them froth up and thicken. Stir this into the flour mixture and mix to form a dough. Leave for at least an hour to cool.

Preheat the oven to 170°C [325°F, Gas 3].

If the mixture has become too hard to roll out, break it up, moisten with a little water and knead into a dough. Roll out thinly – about 3mm [⅛in] – and cut out with a gingerbread man cutter. Make smiling mouths with a spoon and press out circles for eyes and buttons. Press raisins into the holes for buttons (or fill with a drop of melted chocolate or icing after

baking). Lift carefully on to greased baking sheets with a spatula. Bake for about fifteen minutes; remove immediately and cool on a wire rack.

SHORTBREAD

Scottish shortbread is simple but delicious: its superb flavor comes from the butter. This recipe makes eight thick slices.

Ingredients
Metric/Imperial
175g [6oz] plain flour
100g [4oz] butter
50g [2oz] granulated sugar

American
1½ cups enriched flour
½ cup butter
¼ cup sugar

Butter a 20cm [8in] round cake pan or sandwich tin lavishly. Preheat the oven to 180°C [350°F, Gas 4].

Sift the flour into a bowl; cut in the butter, and rub with the fingertips until the mixture resembles coarse breadcrumbs. Stir in the sugar and knead gently until the mixture binds together.

Place in the prepared pan and press out gently to fill (if you don't have a large enough pan, the shortbread can be pressed into a circle on a greased baking sheet). Smooth flat with a palette knife; flute the edges between forefinger and thumb. Cut into eight slices, separating them well, and prick all over.

Bake for about thirty minutes or until golden brown. Turn gently on to a wire rack and leave to cool, then dust with sugar.

Candies

MARZIPAN CANDIES

The basic marzipan mixture can be used to make candies in any shape you like – we've made oranges, apples and assorted fancy shapes. The recipe makes about thirty-six candies.

Ingredients
Metric/Imperial
225g [8oz] ground almonds
100g [4oz] icing sugar
100g [4oz] castor sugar
1 egg, beaten
¼ teaspoon almond essence
For decoration
Orange, red and green food coloring
Whole cloves
Walnuts, almonds or glacé cherries

American
1⅓ cups ground almonds
1 cup confectioners' sugar
½ cup finely granulated sugar
1 egg, beaten
¼ teaspoon almond extract
For decoration
Orange, red and green food coloring
Whole cloves
Walnuts, almonds or candied cherries

Mix all the marzipan ingredients together (1), using just enough egg to make a fairly stiff dough. (If it is too soft the candies will not keep their shape.) Test by rolling a bit into a ball.

Roll out and divide according to the number of different candies you want to make; roll into balls for oranges, apples and covered candies (2).

For oranges, press the ball lightly on the finest side of a grater, then make a slight dent in the top. Brush with orange coloring (3) – it may need watering down a little.

Paint apples green and red and stick a clove in the top for a stalk.

Divide the remaining marzipan as required and mix the coloring, a few drops at a time, into the portions until the right tone is evenly distributed. These pieces can then be rolled into small squares or oblongs, pressed lightly together and cut into whatever shape is wanted with a sharp knife.

To set nuts on candies, coat them underneath with a little marmalade.

1

2

3

Candies

RUM TRUFFLES

These delicious dainties for serving with after-dinner coffee are very easy to make. Ideally they should be put into individual paper cups, otherwise they tend to stick together. We've used rum flavoring, but whisky and coffee are good too. The recipe makes up to twenty-five.

Ingredients

Metric/Imperial
225g [8oz] dark cooking chocolate
2 level tablespoons icing sugar
1½ teaspoons rum or rum essence
25g [1oz] chocolate vermicelli
1 level tablespoon cocoa powder

American
8oz semi-sweet cooking chocolate
2 level tablespoons confectioner's sugar
1½ teaspoons rum or rum extract
1oz chocolate shavings
1 level tablespoon cocoa

Gently melt the chocolate in a bowl set over nearly boiling water. Stir in the sugar and rum. Leave for fifteen minutes until almost set, then scoop out small pieces and roll them into balls in your hands.

Place the chocolate shavings on a plate and roll half the balls in it until covered all over. Roll the remaining balls in the cocoa.

CHOCOLATE SHAPES

Making chocolate shapes is a fun thing for children to do for special occasions like birthdays or Christmas.

Ingredients

1 large bar cooking chocolate
Mold – we used a plastic mold sold in craft shops for casting little clay figures
Cooking oil

Melt the chocolate slowly by placing in a bowl set over nearly boiling water. Brush the mold with oil.

Using a teaspoon quickly fill each mold to the brim with liquid chocolate. Set aside to harden before gently flexing the mold to release the shapes. They can be left as they are or wrapped in gold or silver foil.

TURKISH DELIGHT

Irresistibly sweet and sticky, Turkish Delight is not too difficult to make provided you keep an eagle eye on the temperature of the boiling sugar. This recipe makes thirty-six squares.

Ingredients

Metric/Imperial
450g [1lb] granulated sugar
275ml [½ pint] water
1 teaspoon lemon juice
25g [1oz] gelatine dissolved in
100ml [4fl oz] hot water
½ teaspoon vanilla essence
1 teaspoon rosewater
Red food coloring
50g [2oz] icing sugar
25g [1oz] cornflour

American
2 cups sugar
1¼ cups water
1 teaspoon lemon juice
1oz gelatine dissolved
in ½ cup hot water
½ teaspoon vanilla extract
1 teaspoon rosewater
Red food coloring
½ cup confectioners' sugar
¼ cup cornstarch

Put the sugar, water and lemon juice into a medium-sized heavy pan and heat gently, stirring, until the sugar has dissolved. Increase the heat and bring to the boil. Boil rapidly *without stirring* until a temperature of 116°C [240°F] shows on a sugar thermometer. Remove from heat immediately and plunge pan into cold water to prevent further cooking. (Lacking a sugar thermometer, have ready a saucer of ice-cold water and keep dropping a little syrup into it until the drop forms a soft ball.)

Leave the syrup to cool for ten minutes, then add the dissolved gelatine, vanilla and rosewater and stir vigorously. Add enough drops of coloring to turn the mixture a rich pink; mix well. Pour into a well-greased 15cm [6in] square pan (tin) and leave to cool for at least eight hours.

Dip the pan in hot water and turn out on to a board spread thickly with the sugar and cornflour. Cut into 2.5cm [1in] strips, then into squares, using a long sharp knife dipped in hot water. Toss well so all surfaces are completely coated.

GRANNY'S VANILLA FUDGE

This version of the most popular of all home-made confections is virtually fool-proof – you don't need a sugar thermometer, and there's no guess-work; just follow the directions *exactly*. It tastes delicious and has the grainy texture that fudge should really have. This recipe makes about 700g [1½lb].

Ingredients

Metric/Imperial
450g [1lb] granulated sugar
½ × 383g [13.5oz] can sweetened condensed milk
50g [2oz] butter
100ml [4fl oz] milk
½ teaspoon vanilla essence

American
2 cups sugar
½ × 13.5oz can sweetened condensed milk
¼ cup butter
½ cup milk
½ teaspoon vanilla extract

Grease a 20cm [8in] square pan (tin). Put all the ingredients except vanilla into a medium-sized heavy pan and heat slowly to dissolve the sugar. Bring gradually to a boil and simmer *very gently* for forty minutes, stirring only occasionally to keep from burning. Remove from heat and allow to cool slightly, then add the vanilla and beat for a few minutes until the mixture begins to thicken. Pour into the greased pan. When sufficiently set, mark into squares. Leave until cold before removing from the pan.

Preserves

CONNOISSEUR'S MARMALADE

This is a marmalade for the connoisseur – sharp-tasting and tangy, with a pronounced orange flavor. To turn it into a liqueur marmalade add a miniature of orange liqueur, rum or whisky after boiling. For a dark marmalade use brown sugar. The recipe makes about four jars.

Ingredients
Metric/Imperial
1¾ litres [3 pints] water
1 kilo [2lb] Seville oranges
1 kilo [2lb] granulated sugar
½ teaspoon citric acid or juice of 1 lemon

American
3¾ pints water
2lb bitter oranges
4 cups sugar
½ teaspoon citric acid or juice of 1 lemon

Pour the water over the whole oranges and simmer gently, covered, for a good two hours until very soft. Leave to cool, then cut into chunks or shreds as desired, scooping out and reserving the fiber (pith) and seeds. Put these back into the water and boil for twenty minutes.

Strain out the seeds and fiber and put in the orange peel, sugar and citric acid. Heat very gently until the sugar has dissolved. Increase heat and bring to a rapid boil for twenty minutes or more until the mixture reaches 104°C [220°F] on a sugar thermometer, or until a drop put into ice cold water sets into a ball which wrinkles when pushed with a finger.

Let cool for ten minutes, then ladle into warmed jars. Cover with screw-top lids.
Note Seville oranges have a characteristic bitter flavor ideal for marmalade. They can be bought in cans specially prepared for marmalade making. In Europe they are in season in January and February.

BRANDY POT

Making a brandy pot is a very old method of preserving the luscious fruits of summer as they come along, so that come winter you have a big supply of a deliciously alcoholic fruit cocktail. Decanted into smaller, decorative jars it makes a luxury present.

Ingredients
Metric/Imperial
Fruit: strawberries, raspberries, red and black currants, black cherries, peaches, apricots, plums (225g [8oz] of each)
Sugar
1 bottle inexpensive brandy
1 jar with lid (not metal) large enough to hold about 2 litres [4 pints]

American
Fruit: strawberries, raspberries, blackberries, red currants, black cherries, peaches, apricots, plums, (½lb of each)
Sugar
1 bottle inexpensive brandy
1 jar with lid (not metal) large enough to hold about 5 pints

The fruits listed are those traditionally used – apples and pears can be too bland, bananas go mushy, and oranges tend to dominate. But there's no reason why you shouldn't experiment with other fruit available to you. The end result should be a mixture of fruits, with red color predominating, and a good proportion of firm, identifiable fruit such as cherries so the whole thing doesn't become a mush.

All fruit used should be ripe but not soft. Remove stones from the large fruits and cut into small chunks. (Skin peaches and apricots, plunging them briefly into boiling water first.)

As each fruit comes into season put a layer in the jar and cover with one-third its weight in sugar. Add enough brandy to cover and stir gently. Cover and keep in a cool dark place.

Continue in this way until the jar is full or the fruit season over, stirring gently each time and topping up with brandy. Leave for six weeks after the last addition to mature.

The brandied fruit should be eaten in small quantities as a luxury dessert, with cream and crisp wafers; or serve with vanilla-flavored desserts such as ice-cream, blancmange or junket.

PÂTÉ MAISON

French-style coarse-textured pâté looks very attractive when presented in an earthenware terrine. The fat topping forms a seal, so the pâté will keep for up to a week in a refrigerator; during this time the flavor matures and improves. The recipe makes enough for 4–6 servings.

Ingredients
Metric/Imperial
900g [2lb] belly pork
225g [8oz] pork fat (or use bacon fat)
4 tablespoons dry white wine or cider
12 black peppercorns, crushed
12 juniper berries, crushed
2–4 garlic cloves, crushed
¼ teaspoon grated nutmeg
Pinch ground allspice
Small bay leaves

American
2lb fat pork
½lb salt pork or bacon (slab)
4 tablespoons dry white wine or hard cider
12 black peppercorns, crushed
12 juniper berries, crushed
2–4 garlic cloves, crushed
¼ teaspoon grated nutmeg
Pinch ground allspice
Small bay leaves

Heat the oven to 140°C [275°F, Gas 1].

Remove the rind and any bones from the meat. Cut meat and fat into small cubes and place in a heatproof casserole with all the other ingredients except the bay leaves. Sprinkle with a little salt; mix well, cover and bake for four hours in the center of the oven.

Place a sieve over a large bowl and empty the contents of the casserole into it. Press lightly to drain off excess fat. Turn the meat out on to a large plate and shred it into a paste with two forks.

Pack into a ¾ litre [1½ pint] terrine or earthenware mold. Spoon over melted fat from the bowl to seal completely. Arrange bay leaves attractively on top and set aside to cool.

Preserves

Crafts

Papier Mâché Lampshade

The technique employed for this unusual lampshade – pasting strips of newspaper over a wire frame – can also be adapted to make trays, bowls and similar items, by pasting the strips over an existing object. It is time-consuming, but very simple to do.

Materials
Frame One lampshade frame; masking tape
Papier mâché Newspapers; plain flour; pastry brush; spackling compound (cellulose filler)
Decoration Water-based (emulsion) paint; enamel paint; clear varnish; extra-fine sandpaper

Size
Our lampshade measures about 15cm [6in] high by 30cm [12in] across.

To make a working base, cover frame by winding masking tape around outside from spoke to spoke in overlapping strips.

Tear some newspaper into 2.5cm [1in] strips, tearing with the grain so they come out straight. Divide strips into 5cm [2in] lengths.

Stir a little water into half a cup of flour until mixture is the consistency of cream. Bring to the boil, stirring, then thin down with water until mixture is again of cream consistency.

Dip the paper strips one at a time into the paste until soaked. Apply to the taped frame lengthwise in overlapping bands until no tape is visible.

Add two more layers of strips as follows: spread a coat of paste on first layer with a pastry brush and apply dry paper strips, spread a second coat of paste and apply a last layer of dry

strips, then give a final coat of paste. Let dry overnight.

Repeat the whole strip-laying operation on 4–5 successive days, applying three layers of dry strips each day. End with a layer of larger strips, about 10cm [4in] long, to mold frame well. Let dry thoroughly.

To get a really smooth surface apply a thin coat of spackling compound (cellulose filler). Let dry, then rub down very lightly with extra fine sandpaper.

Apply several coats of emulsion paint as a background, drying between coats.

To decorate paint on a design in enamel paint. If your artistic ability doesn't stretch very far, keep to geometric designs, or trace motifs from the selection on pages 144–9. Outline the design in pencil first, and allow each color to dry before starting another.

Finish with at least 2–3 coats of varnish, the more the better.

Decorative Candles

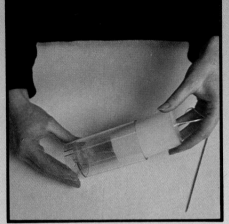

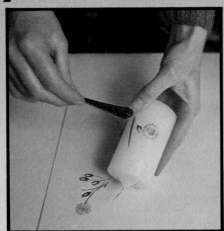

Candlemaking is a fascinating craft with endless possibilities. The beautiful flower and storybook candles are easy to make; from these you can progress to making candles of ever-increasing complexity, in a limitless range of colors, shapes and sizes. Simple candlemaking is great fun for children and gives them good scope for experiment, as failures can be melted down and used again. Children should always be supervised when using hot wax.

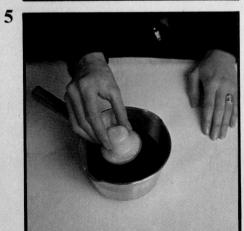

3

Bellis Perennis

Flower Candles

Materials

Paraffin wax 1 kilo [2lb] of wax makes about five medium-sized candles
Stearic acid (stearin) This helps release candle from mold and makes candle opaque. Use one part stearic acid to ten parts wax. Do not use in rubber molds as it rots them
Dyes For coloring use candle color (wax dye) sold in cake form
Perfume A few drops of oil-based perfume can be added if a scented candle is desired
Wicks These must suit the size of the candle. Too big a wick makes the candle smoke
Molds The flower candles were cast in rigid plastic molds, but molds can be improvised from practically anything – cans, glass jars etc – provided the finished candle will come out easily, (alternatively the mold can be cut away or broken)
Other items Kitchen thermometer; small saucepans; asbestos mat; mold stand; wicking or other large needle; bowl or bucket; dried flowers and leaves; mold seal; poster paint

To judge how much wax is needed fill the mold with water and pour it into the saucepan to be used for melting the wax. Make a mark just above the water level to allow for shrinkage of the wax. Dry mold and pan thoroughly.

Prepare the mold, if improvised, by making a small hole in the center bottom for the wick.

Gently melt the wax; a double boiler is ideal, but otherwise use a very low heat and place the pan on an asbestos mat. (Never forget that hot wax can ignite just like boiling fat, so handle with great care; always heat gently and don't overfill the pan. In case of accident, turn off the heat and smother the flames by covering with lid; never use water.)

A thermometer is essential to ensure the wax is at the correct temperature. Wax will melt at about 60°C [140°F], and is ready for initial pouring at 82°C [180°F].

Dip the wick into the melted wax and when cool tie one end on to a small stick long enough to lay across the top of the mold. Thread the other end through the hole in the bottom, pull taut and secure with mold seal, sealing the hole.

Make up the stearic acid following manufacturer's instructions, mixing in the color or dye if using; then add the wax. Raise the heat slightly until pouring temperature is reached.

Place the mold in or on its stand, ensuring it is secure and level. If perfume is desired add now. Carefully pour in the prepared wax. Let stand for a minute to allow air bubbles to rise; tap the mold to help them escape.

For a smooth surface the candle should be cooled in a water bath. This is a bucket or bowl of cold water into which the mold is lowered. Make sure no water goes into the mold and that the water and the wax level are the same. You will have to put a weight on top to stop the mold from floating.

Let candle cool; as it does so, a well appears in the top. Break the surface skin and fill with wax heated to 93°C [200°F]. It may be necessary to do this more than once. Do not let the warm wax rise above the edge of the candle.

When cool slip the candle out of the mold and trim the wick (1).

Before fixing the pressed flowers work out the arrangement. Then place the flowers on the candle and press in position with the back of a fork (2). (The fork can be heated by leaning it against a gently warmed iron.)

The lettering is engraved on the candle with a needle, then painted with poster paint mixed with a drop of liquid detergent, Let dry and remove excess paint with a damp cloth.

Seal the candle by dipping in hot wax at 96°C [205°F] (3). Immerse the candle to the shoulders, leave for three seconds and remove. The candle will go opaque, then clear. If necessary, press down any leaves which may be sticking out and dip again for two seconds.

Storybook Candles

Materials

White candles
Paraffin wax
Other items Red wax dye; white wax crayon; poster paint

Soften the candle by dipping into a pan of paraffin wax heated to 82°C [180°F], at one-minute intervals until it softens. Then pull the wick out and mold the candle into the mushroom shape by pushing it into the palm of your hand to form the dome. Keep dipping it in the hot wax to keep it soft. Push a large needle through the center while still soft and rethread the wick (4).

To make the red cap dip the dome into a small amount of red wax at 82°C [180°F] (5).

To make the white dots add a small piece of white wax crayon to 25g [1oz] of paraffin wax, put into a small metal container and melt over hot water. Dip a needle into the hot mixture and allow drips to fall on the dome to form dots (6).

For doors and windows mark the shapes with a flat stick while the candle is still soft. When hardened fill in the outlines with poster paint mixed with a drop of liquid detergent. When the paint is dry gently rub off excess with a damp cloth. Buff with a dry soft cloth.

Liquid Plastic Casts

A craft made possible by modern technology, liquid plastic casting can be used to make very attractive and unusual gifts, like the paperweights, cufflinks and pendant shown here. Practically anything can be embedded. We have used artificial flowers and Chinese papercuts; other suitable objects are dried flowers and leaves, coins, sea shells, coral, butterflies and the mechanisms of broken clocks and watches.

Materials

Casting (polyester) resin and hardener Types suitable for casting are sold in craft shops
Molds Those sold specially for plastic casting are usually made of polyethylene, but glass, sheet metal, enameled metal and china can also be used
Other items Object(s) for embedding; Mylar plastic film (Melinex foil) or a sheet of glass; wet-and-dry (silicon carbide) abrasive papers; possibly release wax, wax glue, resin dye, plasticine and epoxy resin glue

The basic principle of polyester resin casting is very simple: adding hardener to the casting resin causes it to heat up and cure or set hard. Hardening takes place in two stages. Shortly after hardener is added the resin becomes jelly-like. Then it begins to heat up and turn hard; at average room temperature this takes anything from thirty minutes to four hours or more according to the size of the casting.

It is very important to follow the manufacturer's instructions exactly as to how many drops of hardener to use (this varies from $\frac{1}{2}$–2 per cent by volume, and the *larger* the casting the *less* hardener is required). If too much is used the casting will heat up too quickly and crack; too little and it takes a very long time to harden. Small castings are less prone to cracking, so it's a good idea to start with something small to learn the technique.

Polyethylene molds need no preparation and the finished cast should come out easily as the resin shrinks slightly on hardening. With other molds you must polish the inside with release wax or brush-on liquid mold release.

Objects to be embedded should be clean (polished in the case of coins) and perfectly dry, otherwise whitish discoloration or streakiness occurs. Flowers and leaves always contain moisture, so you must either use artificial ones or sand dry them as described on page 51.

The layer method of embedding objects is the most efficient. Pour in enough resin to half-fill the mold, and after 10–15 minutes prod it every few seconds with a needle to detect when the jelly stage occurs. The item can then be positioned without danger of sinking, and the mold filled with resin. (Less hardener is needed for the second layer, as the first will still be producing heat which helps it to cure.)

After casting cover the surface of the mold with a piece of glass (waxed with release wax) or Mylar (Melinex) sheet as the resin remains sticky if exposed to air. This also gives a smooth finish.

Leave the casting for the full curing time, which varies according to size, so that it is completely hard when taken from the mold. Remove any bumps with a sharp knife or file. Small castings may not require any polishing, but larger ones should be rubbed down with wet-and-dry abrasive paper, starting with a coarse grade and finishing with the finest or with silver polish. The more care you take over polishing the better the finish.

Flower Paperweights

The small paperweight was made using a light bulb as a mold.

First remove the top and element of the bulb by holding the top over a low flame until it becomes loose and twisting it off with a pair of pliers. Then prop up the bulb with a piece of plasticine.

Take a spray of paper flowers, put a safety pin through the stalks, and rest it on the top of the mold with the flowers hanging downwards.

Pour the resin over the flowers (1) and let cure for about twenty-four hours (2).

To remove wrap in a piece of cloth and tap it on the table; this breaks the glass and releases the paperweight (3).

The polygonal paperweight is made in a two-part polyethylene candle mold. Seal the two parts together with wax glue, and make as above.

Cufflinks and Pendant

These are made in layers in a polyethylene resin-casting mold. Warm the mold and pour in a very small amount of resin, just enough to half-fill it, using 2 per cent hardener.

About fifteen minutes later, when it gels, introduce the swirling color by drawing on the surface with a cocktail stick dipped in resin dye.

After ten minutes fill the mold to the top with resin. Cover with Mylar (Melinex) sheet.

When they have set, polish. Fix on links with epoxy resin glue. Drill hole in pendant for chain.

Chinese Papercut Paperweight

This colorful paperweight was made with one Chinese papercut, using the layer method.

Round and Hexagonal Paperweights

These are more difficult to make, being larger.

To cast the round one, you need a 10cm [4in] diam. candle mold. Polish the inside with release wax. Use a minimum amount of hardener ($\frac{1}{2}$ per cent) to avoid cracking. If you want a crack effect, cool it quickly with cool air or an ice pack.

The hexagonal one is made in a hexagonal candle mold. Resin dye is mixed with the resin before it is poured in to give the smoky effect.

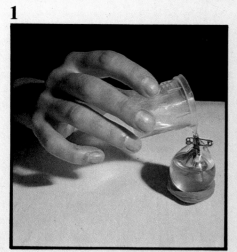

Needlecase, Pincushion and Glasses' Case

2

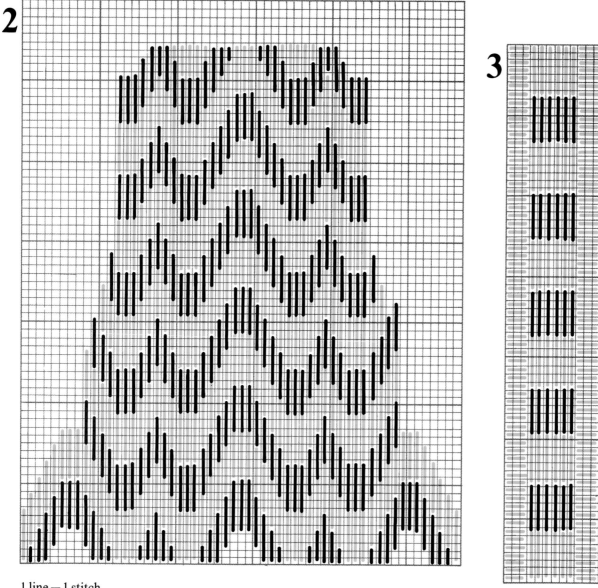

3

1 line = 1 stitch
a–b = pincushion width
a–c = needlecase width

1

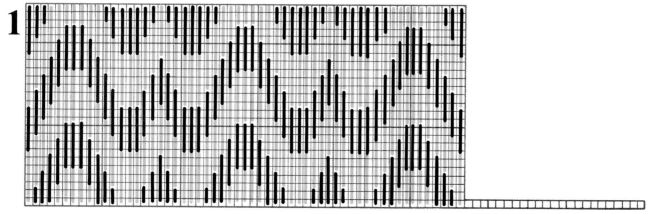

a   b   c

Bargello or Florentine stitch is one of the fastest and easiest as well as most attractive needlepoint stitches. The zigzag rows using two or more tones of the same color give an impression of flames or waves. We have used greens and browns, but it's fun to experiment with your own color selection.

Needlecase

Materials
Single thread canvas 18-mesh or 18 threads per 2.5cm [1in], one piece 15 × 13cm [6 × 5in]
Felt One piece 12 × 10cm [5 × 4in] to match one of the darker wool colors
Wool fabric Scraps of loosely woven fabric
Tapestry yarn Five skeins: two tones of one color and three of the other
Tapestry needle

Each stitch covers six threads of canvas. Following diagram 1, work the pattern until you have an oblong with seven complete rows. (We used two shades of green, three of brown, finishing with two of green.) Trim canvas to within 1cm [⅜in] of worked area and fold seams under. Fold seam

allowance to make felt the same size as the worked canvas. Overcast (oversew) felt to canvas as neatly as possible.

Cut three pieces of wool fabric 9.5 × 6.5cm [3¾ × 2½in] and trim with pinking shears. Sew to center inside cover. Fold needlecase in half and press.

Pincushion

Materials
Canvas As above, one piece 13 × 13cm [5 × 5in]
Felt One piece 10 × 10cm [4 × 4in]
Tapestry wool As above
Tapestry needle
Stuffing

Following diagram 1, work the pattern until you have a square with seven complete rows. Trim, turn and attach felt as for needlecase at three sides. Stuff pincushion and overcast the remaining side.

Glasses' Case

Materials
Canvas As above, one piece 13 × 54cm [5 × 21in]
Tapestry wool Eleven skeins: five tones

of one color, five tones of the other, one extra skein of one tone for binding
Tapestry needle
Note If you make the glasses' case you will have enough yarn left over to make the other two items.

Following diagram 1, work the pattern for forty-five rows, then decrease to make flap (diagram 2). Work flap band (diagram 3). Trim band and case to within three threads of worked area.

Overcast long edges of band with double thickness of tapestry yarn. Overcast straight end of main piece and flap. Fold main piece over, right side out, leaving flap free, and overcast along the sides, attaching the band 1cm [⅜in] from the top.

Belt Bazaar

BELT BAZAAR

The choice of belts has been made to suit every personality and life style. To make, the leather and suede ones are fairly ambitious, as is the silver tapestry evening belt; but the appliquéd felt and tape measure belts demand only ordinary skill on the sewing machine, while the curtain tape and stenciled webbing belts are well within the scope of children. You don't have to follow our designs exactly – be adventurous and create your own variations.

Leather Belt

Materials
Ready-cut belt length 5cm [2in] wide and 15cm [6in] longer than person's waist
Leather thonging 5 × 1m [1yd] different colors
Other items 5cm [2in] buckle with prong; clear glue; spray-on shoe leather polish
Tools Ruler and knitting needle: 2.5cm [1 in] chisel and a mallet; sharp craft knife; harness (spring-type thonging) needle; belt punch.

With ruler and knitting needle score a very faint line down the belt 1.2cm [½in] from one side, starting 8cm [3in] from one end and finishing 25cm [10in] from the other. Mark this line off into 1.2cm [½in] sections. Punch slits at these marked positions; a chisel does the job quickly and efficiently, but it can be done with the sharp knife.

Thread the needle with one of the thongings and 'darn' it through the slits all down the belt, leaving the ends on the wrong side. Repeat with the other colors. Go over the work with the knitting needle and push the thonging into place where necessary to form an even pattern. Trim ends and glue down.

Punch a hole 4cm [1½in] from the shortest plain end of the belt and thread on buckle. Fold back surplus leather and glue down. Shape other end into a curved point with the knife, then punch holes at about 4cm [1½in] intervals down the center.

Spray with leather polish and buff to a soft shine.

Suede Belt

Materials

Suede Scraps in different colors
Other items 5cm [2in] buckle with
prong; clear glue
Tools Sharp scissors; belt punch;
2.5cm [1in] chisel and a mallet or
sharp craft knife

Make a pattern in stiff cardboard using
the outlined shape in diagram 1 (actual
size). Iron the suede scraps carefully on
the wrong side if crumpled. Use the
cardboard template and a ballpoint
pen to draw about twenty shapes in
toning colors on the back of the suede.

For the buckle end, cut one shape
following the solid blue shape on
diagram 1; punch a hole in the center.
For the other end, cut a strip of suede
40cm [16in] long by 5cm [2in] wide and
use the template to round off the ends.
Fold in half to find the center and use
the template to shape this in the same
way as the centers of the rounded
shapes.

The finished belt should be about
15cm [6in] longer than the person's
waist measurement. Five shapes
measure about 20cm [8in] long, and
the end tab measures the same, so
estimate how many shapes to use and
arrange them in a pleasing color
sequence.

Thread the small section with the hole
on to the buckle and glue together. Use
the chisel and mallet, or a sharp knife,
to cut a slit in the curved end in the
position shown on the diagram.
Thread the first round through this slit,
glue together and continue in this way
until all the rounds are used up. Finish
with the tab strip. Glue it together and
then punch holes down the middle at
about 4cm [1½in] intervals.

Teenager's Belt

Materials

Pleating (curtain heading) tape 1m
[1yd]
Other items 1m [1yd] cord; eight brass
curtain rings

Cut a 15cm [6in] length from the tape.
Turn back the ends 1cm [⅜in] and secure
with zigzag stitch to form channels for
the cording.

Cut a second piece of tape to waist
measurement less 15cm [6in]. Turn back
the ends and stitch as before.

Divide cord roughly in half (do not
cut) and thread through channels as
shown in diagram 2, starting at **a.**
Knot each end of cord on to a curtain
ring. Thread remaining rings on to the
loops in the tape for hanging mascots
and charms.

.... sewing line

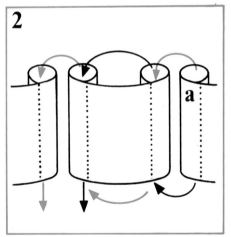

Peasant Belt

Materials

Felt Two pieces 15cm [6in] wide ×
waist measurement; scraps for
decorating
Other items One piece heavy iron-
on interfacing same size as felt; 1m
[1yd] cord; wooden beads
Note In diagram 3, one square = 2·5cm
[1in]

Fold the interfacing in half widthwise
and draw the belt shape (diagram 3) on
it in soft pencil. The width
measurements are 12cm [4½in] at center
front; 5cm [2in] on the straight, and
8cm [3in] at center back. Length is
half waist measurement less 1cm [⅜in].

Cut out and iron to one piece of the
felt. Place second piece underneath;
baste together, stitching closely around
interfacing. Trim away surplus felt to
within 1cm [⅜in] of the interfacing.

Machine stitch all around close to the
interfacing, leaving an opening at
lower center back. Trim off seam
allowance, clipping into seam at inner
corners and cutting diagonally across
outside corners. Turn right side out,
press well and slip-stitch opening
closed.

Cut out felt shapes to decorate; sew
on with zigzag stitch, or glue on with
rubber-based adhesive.

Use a rotary (eyelet) punch to make
five holes down each side of center
front. Finish with eyelets, or buttonhole
stitch. Lace the cord through, and
finish each end with wooden beads,
knotted on.

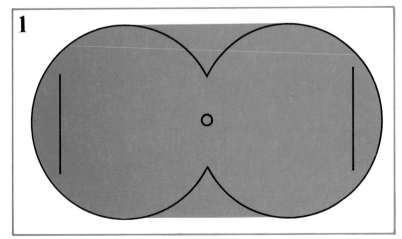

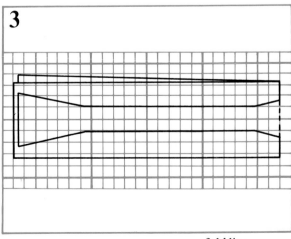

fold line - - - - - - -

Silver Tapestry Belt

Materials

Single thread canvas 20 threads per 2.5cm [1in], one piece 100 × 12cm [36 × 4¾in]
Pearl cotton No. 5 One (10g [½oz]) ball gray; two balls white
Silver lurex thread Equivalent amount to gray
Other items 4cm [1½in] buckle without prong; 100 × 3cm [1yd × 1¼in] lightweight interfacing

Find the center of the piece of canvas and work the pattern from there as shown in diagram 4. Work one end in a V-shape as indicated. Following the pattern, leave 1.2cm [½in] at each end of the embroidery. Iron or sew on the interfacing to the wrong side of the embroidery.

Fold one long side of the canvas over to cover the interfacing and baste in place. Fold under a 1.2cm [½in] seam allowance on the other side and hem in place along the center of the wrong side of belt. Fold under seam allowance at each short end and sew.

Put straight end of belt through buckle; turn under and stitch firmly.

Weight Watcher's Belt

Materials

Belting (petersham) 1m × 4cm [1yd × 1½in]
Other items One tape measure; buckle with prong to fit; rotary (eyelet) punch

Turn over 6mm [¼in] at one end of the belting, then fold over the corners so that the tape measure fits neatly into the space. Using a small zigzag stitch, machine stitch the tape measure into place along the full length of the belting. Cut tape off where it extends beyond the belting.

Fold the belting over the buckle bar, punching a hole for the prong with a rotary (eyelet) punch. Stitch firmly into place.

Punch holes down the center at the other end of the belt, and finish with eyelets or buttonhole stitch.
Note If you don't think the wearer will want to advertise her waist measurement to the world, put the starting end of the tape measure on the tab end of the belt, as we have done here. If you do, make the belt up in reverse, starting at the buckle end.

Stenciled Webbing Belts

Materials

Upholstery webbing Natural-colored 1m × 5cm [1yd × 2in]
Other items Buckle without prong to fit; newspaper; blotting paper; thin cardboard; fabric paints; stencil brush

Wash and rinse webbing; iron when fairly damp, then let dry. Set up a work table in a good light and pad the surface with layers of newspaper covered with a large sheet of blotting paper. Read the manufacturer's instructions before using fabric paint.

Our belts are mainly done by stenciling on simple triangles and squares. You can use any shape you want, so long as they are kept simple; geometric shapes are generally the most successful.

Cut the required stencil shape from thin cardboard, using a sharp craft knife, having cardboard the same width as the belt. Use the stencil first to mark the design lightly in pencil on the belt at the intervals required. Then hold it firmly in place and apply the color with a stencil brush (a stiff, flat-ended brush).

Blue and orange belt Stencil all the triangles in one color first; wipe the stencil clean, and reverse to print the others. Then cut a 2cm [¾in] diam. stencil to print the circles (or use a dowel rod or cork dipped into the paint).

Green and yellow belt Use a cardboard stencil for the squares and paint yellow lines in afterwards freehand.

Red triangle belt Place triangle stencil on the edge of webbing at about 1cm [⅜in] intervals. Print along one edge first, then along the opposite side to get a zigzag effect.

When belt design is complete, leave to dry thoroughly, preferably hanging up. Fix the color with a hot iron following the manufacturer's instructions. Finish by sewing buckle on to one end of belt length and hemming other end.

4

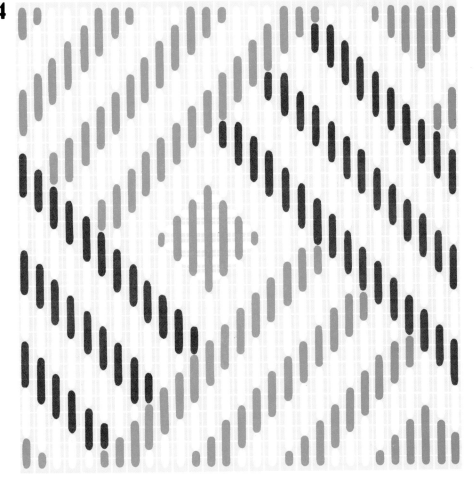

white — white
silver — silver
gray — gray

1 line = 1 stitch

Potato Printing

These highly original covers are produced by very simple means: with fabric paints, a potato and two pastry cutters

Materials
Plain or checked fabric According to size and number of pillows
Fabric paint Any which can be used on natural or synthetic fabrics. (We used Dylon Color-fun.)
Pastry cutters Small size: one heart and one circle
Other items Newspaper; roll of paper towels; two felt squares; shallow dish: large potato; sharp knife; paintbrush; masking tape; pillow forms (cushion pads)

If the fabric is new wash, dry and iron it. Cut out the covers, allowing an additional 1.2cm [½in] all around for seams.

Cover the working surface with a wad of newspaper, lay fabric on top and secure with tape. Work out your design on a similar-sized sheet of paper, then lightly mark the position of the design on the fabric with a soft pencil and ruler. (These guide lines can be erased when the paint has dried.)

To make the printing blocks, cut the potato in half and press a pastry cutter firmly into the center of each cut surface. Slice away potato from outside the cutter (1); remove cutter.

For each printing pad, place a felt square in a shallow dish and coat liberally with fabric paint. Blot the printing block with paper towels (to remove natural moisture produced by the potato) and press on to the felt until well coated. Then press firmly on to the fabric (2). Practise getting a good, even print on scrap fabric.

Work from the top of the fabric down to avoid smudging the motifs, pressing the block firmly on to the felt pad each time before printing. Blot the potato from time to time to keep the surface dry, and add more paint to the pad as needed.

Follow the manufacturer's instructions for fixing the paint with a hot iron (3). Make up fabric into an attractive cover, plain or piped as preferred.

1
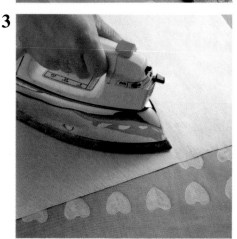

2

3

Embroidered Owls

Our delightful family of owls is an exercise in truly creative embroidery, using thick yarns on burlap (hessian). No two owls ever come out quite the same – as you can see from the picture, each one has its own distinctive personality.

Materials (for each owl)
Burlap (hessian) or other coarse fabric One piece 30 × 50cm [12 × 20in]
Heavy yarn Browns, grays and fawns in textured tweed effect
Fine yarn or thick thread Beige, cream and fawn
Lead soldering wire One piece 38cm × 3mm [15 × ⅛in]
Beads Two black beads for eyes, one long pearl bead for beak
Other items Synthetic stuffing; small piece of forked tree branch for perch; small nail
Note In diagram 1, one square = 1.2cm [½in]

Copy the owl shape (diagram 1) on to a piece of paper, making it about 20cm [8in] high for large owl. Transfer the drawing twice on to coarse fabric, using carbon paper.

When embroidering the shapes make sure the two halves will fit together to make a complete owl when finished. The basic technique is to embroider all over the back, tail and sides of front with big stitches, using the thick yarns, and to embroider the breast and face in a fine stitch such as stem stitch, using the fine yarn or thread. But this can be varied at will; for example,

one of our owls has its breast decorated with brown beads.

Cut around shapes, leaving a small seam allowance. Sew together leaving an opening at the tail for stuffing. Stuff firmly, but not too hard; sew up tail.

Divide the wire into six pieces (three for each leg). Loop over one another to make legs and claws (diagram 2). Wrap light-colored thread around legs and claws, leaving tips uncovered, binding the joint very firmly where the wires cross. Bend leg up and press into body; splay the claws

1

2

Owl shape for front and back (cut 2)

out. Put in eye and beak beads.

Clean the branch, if necessary, and make sure it will sit level. Place owl's claws on the fork so that they grip, and arrange the body attractively on the branch. Hammer a nail through the tail to secure the bird to the perch.

Bowls of Bulbs

An attractive bowl filled with flowering
bulbs is a gift which almost anyone
will appreciate. Prices of bulbs vary
considerably, so you can make the
gift modest or magnificent.

Materials (1)
Container Any kind of bowl or pot,
whether it is plastic, china,
earthenware or metal, is suitable
provided it is deep enough for root
development. Drainage holes are not
required when using bulb fiber.
Bulb fiber Available in small bags
Bulbs Sold singly or in groups
Other items Pieces of broken pot or
china, or pebbles for drainage; moss,
for decoration (optional); charcoal
chips
Hyacinths are the most popular bulbs,
with their strongly scented flowers.
Daffodils, narcissi and tulip bulbs are
cheaper, and lend themselves to mass
display; crocuses look enchanting
planted in special crocus pots with holes
through which the flowers appear.

Start by soaking the bulb fiber for
several hours until moist enough to
stick together in a loose ball when
squeezed. Plant the bulbs in the early
autumn. As the fiber does not nourish
the bulbs, but only supports them and

holds water, they can be planted almost touching so as to give a mass display in one container.

If you are using a pot with drainage holes you should put a few pebbles or pieces of broken clay or china in the bottom first (2). If there are no drainage holes, it is a good idea to put a little charcoal in the bottom of the bowl, as this helps to keep the fiber sweet.

To plant hyacinth bulbs put enough fiber in the bowl for the tops of the bulbs to peep above the rim. The tips of smaller bulbs should be about 2.5cm [1in] below the rim.

Stand the bulbs on the fiber, closely packed together (3). Pack more fiber in between and around them, firming

it well. Decorate with moss (4).

Level the fiber off about 1cm [$\frac{3}{8}$in] below the rim of the bowl. When watering, fill the bowl to the rim and leave the water to soak in.

Plant daffodil or tulip bulbs in two layers for a mass display. Place the first layer halfway down in a large, deep pot. Almost cover with fiber, then place another layer of bulbs in the spaces. Fill up with fiber. The bulbs will grow and flower together.

Plant crocus bulbs in a crocus pot so that the tips just show through the holes in the sides and the top.

When you have planted the bulbs put in a label bearing the name of the flower and the date of planting. Put the bowl in a cool place such as a garage or shed, covering it with newspaper or black plastic sheeting.

1

2

3

Leave for 2–3 months, during which time the bulbs should fill the bowl with roots. Check from time to time to see if more water is required.

It usually takes about 3–4 weeks for bulbs to flower once they have been brought indoors. Keep them in half-light first for about a week until the growth looks green and healthy, and make sure that they are not near an open fire, radiator or hot air vent.

4

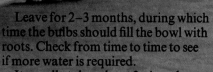

Bouquet Garni Tree

This little yellow rose tree makes a charming present for a keen cook to put on her window sill – the pink gingham bags hold bouquet garni, and the leaves are real bay leaves.

Materials

For the tree 30cm [12in] dowel rod; 10cm [4in] diam. florists' foam ball; small flower pot; spackling compound (cellulose filler); peat; 100×2cm [$36 \times \frac{3}{4}$in] brown crêpe paper
For paper roses One package yellow crêpe paper; one pack medium-size floral wires
For bouquet garni bags One piece gingham 30×115cm [12×45in]; one pack hair pins; button thread; bouquet garni mixture (bay leaves, parsley, thyme); whole bay leaves

Tree

Insert the dowel rod into the foam ball. Make diagonal snips along one edge of the brown crêpe paper (this gives a thorn effect), bind around the dowel and secure end with transparent tape.

Make a stiff mixture of spackle (cellulose filler) and water and fill flower pot to within two-thirds of the top. Insert dowel in center and let set overnight. Finish with a layer of peat.

Roses

Cut a 7.5cm [3in] strip off the yellow crêpe paper (do not unwind). Keeping paper folded, trim off corners and snip out a V-shape in center to form petals (diagram 1). Unwind the strip and gently stretch curved edges of each petal between thumb and forefinger to give a rolled edge (diagram 2). Cut off about a ten-petal strip and begin to form a rose. Wind the first petal curving inwards to form center, then change direction so petals curve outwards. Arrange the petals, keeping a firm grip with left hand until the whole strip is used (diagrams 3 and 4).

Take a floral wire and firmly bind it around base of flower, finishing with ends pointing downwards to form a prong. Trim away surplus paper so rose will sit flat against the ball.

Make eleven flowers and arrange over the ball: one on top, four around the middle, four in lower half and two on each side of top.

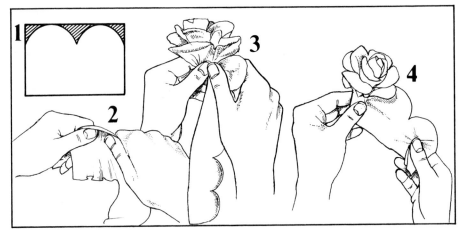

Bouquet garni bags

With pinking shears cut ten 13cm [5in] diam. circles from the gingham. Place about a teaspoon of bouquet garni mixture in center and tie up with button thread, binding neatly around neck of bag.

Slip hair pins around the necks and insert bags in between the flowers on the ball. Fill any spaces with bay leaves.

Baby Mobile

Here's an unusual present that will keep a young baby happy for hours – the gaily decorated egg shells respond to every tiny current of air, creating an ever-changing, ever-moving pattern. The mobile should be hung out of the child's reach, with plenty of room to revolve.

Materials

Six large eggs Remove contents as shown below
Poster paints and varnish
Mobile wires Two 10cm [4in]; one 20cm [8in]; one 25cm [10in]
Other items Thin darning needle long enough to pass right through egg; button thread; six small beads; clear glue; lengths of wire; florist's foam

First blow six eggs as follows: with a darning needle, pierce a hole in

each end of the egg. At the narrow end, use the needle to enlarge the hole to about the size of a pea. Hold the egg over a small bowl. Blow strongly through the small hole to expel the contents into the bowl. Rinse the shells out with water. Leave overnight in a warm place to dry out inside.

Decorate the egg shells with bright, simple designs like the ones in the picture. Pencil the design on first, then color in the shapes with poster paint, letting each color dry thoroughly before adding the next. For speed, paint the shells piece-meal, using all one color first; by the time the last one has had its first color, the first should be ready for its next color. To dry, place the shells on lengths of wire inserted in florists' foam or plasticine. When completely painted and thoroughly dry, spray carefully with varnish, following manufacturer's instructions. Let dry.

Cut six lengths of button thread about 40cm [16in] long; thread through each shell. Knot a bead firmly at the large-hole end and pull up inside shell to rest under small hole.

To assemble first take one of the short wires and tie a shell to each hooked end so they hang at slightly different levels as in the picture. Knot threads securely to wire and trim surplus, leaving about 1cm [⅜in]. Knot a short length of thread to center of wire and attach the other end to something like a hanging lampshade, where it can freely revolve. Move the thread along the wire until it is perfectly balanced.

Make up the second short wire in the same way but with only one shell; the other hook takes the already made-up section. Adjust the hanging thread as before, making sure shells do not collide as they move around. Fix the medium-sized wire in the same way.

The final, longest wire has a long-threaded shell on one end, a short-threaded one in the center and the rest of the mobile at the other end. Balance as before; the hanging thread and the short-threaded shell must both be adjusted until the wire hangs horizontally.

Finish the free ends of thread by sticking to the main part.

Macramé Dog Leash and Collar

If you've never done macramé before, making a leash and collar for your pet is a simple thing to begin with. First make the leash, then go on to the collar. But before starting, study the diagrams closely and practise the knots.

Leash

Materials
Strong fine twisted string or medium cotton seine twine 7.5m [8¼yd] dark color; 11m [12¼yd] light color.
One dog leash fastener
Equipment One piece bulletin board about 30 × 45cm [12 × 18in]; T-pins; large bulldog clip; rubber bands

Size
102 × 2cm [40 × ¾in]

Cut the light-colored twine into one 7.5m [8¼yd] length and one 3.5m [4yd]. To make, pin the dog lead fastener to the middle of the board and prop the board against the edge of a table. Double the one dark and two light threads in half and set on to the ring of the fastener with Lark's Head Knots (diagram 1), with the shorter light thread in the center and the dark thread to the right. Tie the bulldog clip around your waist and use to hold the core (center four) threads taut. Wind the outer knotting threads into figure-eight hanks to make them short enough to work with; secure with a rubber band.

The pattern is worked in alternate lengths of square (flat) knots and half knots, the variation in color being achieved by changing over the knotting threads at intervals.

Using the first (light) thread and the last (dark) thread as knotting threads, work 10cm [4in] of square (flat) knots (diagram 2). Combine the light knotting thread with the core threads. Using both the dark threads as knotting threads, work 6cm [2½in] of half knots (diagram 3). (The half knot is simply the first step of the square (flat) knot, and twists naturally into a spiral.)

Repeat first section once and second section once. Then work as first section for 31cm [12in] and as second section for 10cm [4in].

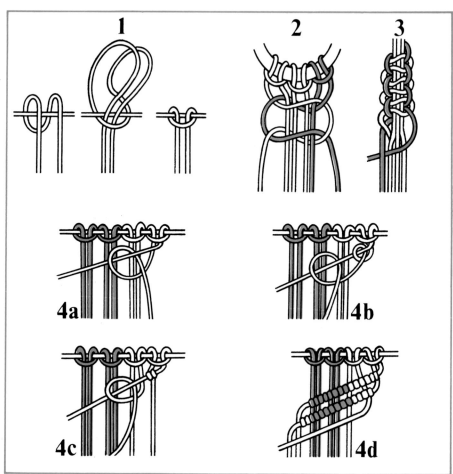

50

Change over the two long light and dark threads so that the longest in each case becomes the knotting thread and work as first section for 10cm [4in].

To divide for handle, divide threads into two groups each containing one long light, one long dark and one short light thread. Using the single short light thread as the core in each group, make 15cm [6in] of square (flat) knots, keeping the dark thread on the right.

Lay the two sides of the handle together and make an overhand knot (simple loop) over all threads. Trim ends 15cm [6in] below knot.

Collar

Materials
Strong fine twisted cotton string or medium cotton seine twine 8m [9yd] dark; 8m [9yd] light
Buckle 2.5cm [1in] bar
D-ring 2.5cm [1in] flat side
Equipment As for leash; clear glue

Size
38 × 2.5cm [15 × 1in]

Cut the light and dark twine in half. Double and set on to the buckle bar with Lark's Head knots (diagram 1), two dark threads at left, two light threads at right.

The pattern is diagonal double half-hitching, which consists simply of laying the last thread diagonally to the left over the other seven (diagram 4) and working double half-hitches on it.

After working about 12cm [5in], half-hitch the next row over the flat bar of the D-ring. Continue until collar is the desired length (more twine would be needed for a larger collar).

To finish, make an overhand knot (simple loop) over each thread, close to the cording. Cut ends and brush knots with clear glue.

Diagram 4
a Use the last right-hand thread as a leader, held taut in left hand. Loop next thread over and under taut thread making one half-hitch.
b Tighten loop, push along to end. Make another half-hitch with *same* thread over taut thread, completing double half-hitch.
c Pick up each thread in turn across the row and make a double half-hitch on to the taut thread, thus making a row of cording.
d When last thread is worked, return to right side and start again with the extreme right-hand cord as leader.

Dried Flower Bouquet

A selection of dried flowers, grasses, seedheads and leaves makes a welcome present for a keen flower arranger.

Materials
Flowers Helichrysum (everlasting flower), Limonium (sea lavender), Achillea (yarrow), etc.
Seed pods Lunaria (honesty), Physalis alkekengii (Chinese lantern), Scirpus (bulrush) etc.
Grasses Barley, wheat, oats, Cortaderia (Pampas grass) etc.
Leaves Beech or any smooth variety such as oak, poplar, sweet chestnut etc.
Other items According to method

Air drying
Most flowers, seed pods and grasses are dried hanging downwards to encourage straight stems. Pick them as soon as fully developed, on a dry day and in the afternoon when dew has dried. Strip flowers of their leaves; tie up in small bunches, and hang upside down in a warm dry room for a week or two – when ready the flowers will feel dry but not brittle

Borax and sand
This method is for drying large single blooms. You'll need a shallow box and one part borax to two parts dry white sand. Put some sand mixture in the bottom of the box; place a flower on it, head down, and support by covering with more of the mixture. Continue, making sure heads don't touch. Store in a cool, dark place for two weeks; pour away sand and clean flowers with a soft brush.

Glycerine
This is the method for preserving foliage. Use one part glycerine to two parts water. Prepare the foliage by removing any damaged leaves and hammering the bottom of the stem to split the bark. Then stand in a jar of the glycerine solution for about two weeks; the leaves will change color and feel firm but not brittle.

Dyeing
To dye flowers use a plastic bucket, multi-purpose dye, and very hot water. This will produce delicate pastel shades.

Canalware

Take a piece of chipped old enamelware and transform it into an unusual gift by painting it in the style used by Britain's canal boat people for generations. It looks elaborate but is quite simple to do as the designs are built up by repeating the basic motif, the formalized rose, and adding leaves, bands of color and stylized daisies. Any sort of enamelware can be painted – best sources of supply are inexpensive china stores, second-hand places and sales.

Materials

Enamelware
Gloss enamel paint 125ml [¼ pint] can of dark green for background; smaller cans of lime green, yellow, red, white and black for decorating
Other items Small household paint brush; masking tape; China marker (Chinagraph) pencil; small, medium and large pointed artist's brushes; brush cleaner

First make sure the enamelware is clean, dry and grease-free. If painting several items work each step on all of them at once, rather than completing one item at a time.

Paint the items all over the outside in dark green, except handles or knobs. Let them dry in a dust-free place for at least six hours; preferably overnight. Paint handles or knobs black and let them dry again.

Before starting to decorate the items, practise painting the motifs shown in the diagrams on thick paper or white cardboard. You will find that the basic leaf and petal shapes can be created simply by placing a pointed brush down in just the right way, filled with just the right amount of paint. Make the dots for stamens and daisies with the tip of the brush. The size of the leaf, petal or dot depends on the size of the brush.

The scale of the design will vary according to whether the item is a small mug or a large watering can. But generally make the red bands 2cm [¾in] wide, with a 6mm [¼in] yellow band on each side, and the circle forming the base for the roses about 4.5cm [1¾in] diam.

The diagrams show how the rose design is built up in steps; always allow the paint to dry thoroughly between each step. If you are not satisfied with a shape you can quickly wipe it off with a cloth dampened (not saturated) with brush cleaner.

Decide where to place the red band on each item, using our pieces as a guide – a large item might need two bands. If the item is straight-sided, you can mark a level line with masking tape; otherwise use China marker pencil. Also pencil on the circles where each rose is to go.

First paint the red band and red circles. (If you feel you need a guide for the roses with red petals, paint black circles where these are to go.) Then paint the yellow bands.

Next paint the rose petals: some yellow, some white and some red; the lime green leaves and white daisy petals. Follow up with three yellow dots on each rose for stamens, one dot in the center of each daisy, and yellow lines for leaf veins.

Finally paint a red border around the rim of each item.

Leave the completed work for several days to dry before handling or putting on lids.

Enamelware painted in this way is suitable for light use – you can make coffee or tea in the pots, and drink it from the mugs – but handle with care to avoid chipping. (If old enamelware is chipped inside it should be used for display only.)

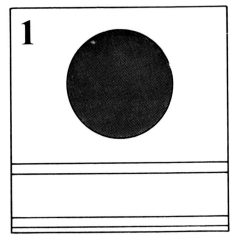

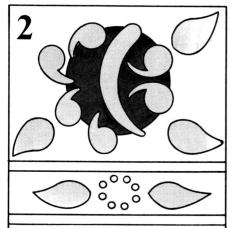

'Silent Night' Advent Calendar

With this Advent calendar, little children can see how close Christmas is getting by the number of stars sparkling in the sky – every day in December they reveal another one, culminating with the big guiding star above the stable. Finally, on Christmas Eve, they open the stable doors to reveal a simple but charming Nativity scene.

Materials

Cardboard Stiff and lightweight
Paper Dark blue, golden yellow, olive green and dark brown construction (cartridge) paper; light brown wood-grain
Thin balsa wood For roof and manger
Items for figures 2.5cm [1in] and 2cm [¾in] polystyrene foam or wooden balls for heads; lightweight white paper; blue and white facial tissues; pipe cleaner; two large gold sequins
Adhesives Re-usable gum-type (Blu-Tack or Sticky-tack); transparent tape; paper paste; all-purpose clear glue
Other items Twenty-three small stick-on silver stars; rhinestones, sequins, etc for central star; dried grasses; two large and two small wooden beads; glitter, silver braid and two small bells; strong thread and fine cord
Note In diagrams, 1 square = 2cm [¾ in]

Cut a 30cm [12in] diam. circle of stiff cardboard for the background. Paste blue paper on front, wood-grain on back. Draw stable outline (diagram 1) on wood-grain paper, and cut out. Paste it on background as in picture. Cut 1cm [⅜in] strips of wood-grain paper, grain running opposite way, and paste over sides (a). Add strips of dark brown paper for beams and step (b). Draw hinges with a felt-tipped pen.

To make doors, with a sharp knife cut across top and bottom and down center. Make pin-holes at outer corners of doors; score side of each door between holes, then turn to back and carefully cut *part-way only* through cardboard between holes. Gently push doors open from back. Make holes for handles and fix a large bead outside, small one inside, joined with glue and a sliver of matchstick.

Cut roof pieces from balsa wood; sprinkle glitter along top edges before gluing in place.

Scatter stars at random over the sky, with one at top center over stable. Build this one up with rhinestones or sequins as in picture.

For the frame, cut olive paper (diagram 2). Cut out center circle 9cm [3½in] diam. and score along broken lines (for folds). Glue grass around inner edge of circle. Crease and bend inner folds *up* and outer folds *back*. Tape sections a to back of calendar, folds level with cut edges of door opening.

For the stable interior, cut yellow paper (diagram 3) and score along broken lines. Cut a separate base section (shaded); back with thin cardboard, and glue to main piece. Glue grass to back as in picture. Crease folds and bend top, sides and base *up*, tabs a back. Fold tabs b over top and under base; fix temporarily with paper clips.

Figures and Manger

Virgin Mary Cut a 14cm [5½in] diam. semi-circle of white paper; remove a 1cm [⅜in] semi-circle at center. Twist into a cone of double thickness paper, straight edges level; glue the join. Fix head ball on a 5cm [2in] length of pipe cleaner, insert into cone, and tape inside. Fold a 20cm [8in] diam. circle of blue tissue in half, drape over head, and glue lightly to lower edge of

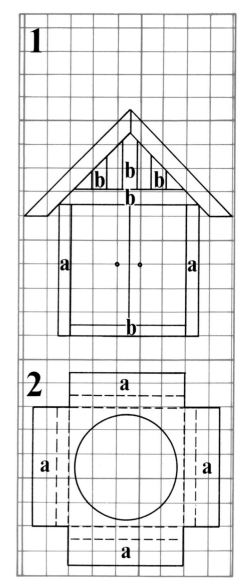

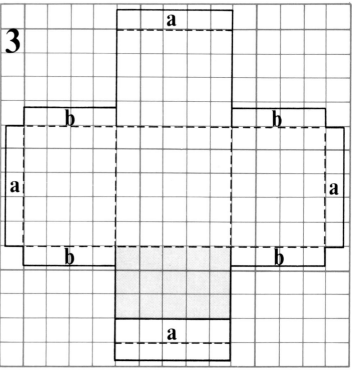

cone. Bend head forward and fix halo (large sequin) at back.

Baby Jesus Bend a 4cm [1½in] length of pipe cleaner in half; fix head ball on cut ends. Fold a 15cm [6in] diam. circle of white tissue in half, drape over head and wrap closely around body. Fix halo.

Manger Cut balsa wood to make sides 5.5 × 3cm [2¼ × 1¼in] and ends 3cm [1¼in] square. Tape lower edges of sides together then bend up and glue between ends in a V-shape. Fill with grass.

Finishing

Arrange figures in stable and glue down. Position interior behind green frame, fitting inside edge over frame: tape yellow tabs a over green tabs a. Glue tabs b lightly in place. Hang bells from bottom of stable.

Cut twenty-two small square 'diamonds' in blue paper; number each, and fix at random over small stars with a blob of re-usable adhesive. Similarly cover large star. Close stable doors and secure with thread. Number another small diamond '24' and fix over thread.

Sprinkle glitter over foreground and glue silver braid around edge of circle. Fix loop of cord at center top to hang up.

Note Once stable doors are open the calendar should be hung in a window or placed with a lamp behind it to illuminate the Nativity scene.

String Things

A desk 'tidy' and plant pot covers in glowing colors can be simply made by covering cardboard tubes and plastic containers with random-dyed coarse string. The idea can be applied to any kind of container, and can also be done on a larger scale, for example to revive a tired old tin wastepaper basket.

Materials

Coarse parcel string 10m [11yd] for desk 'tidy'; as required for plant pot covers
Cold water dye Orange and pink with appropriate fixative.
Clear glue
For plant pot covers Discarded plastic containers
For desk 'tidy' Cardboard sheet, two cardboard tubes

Wind the string into a hank and tie loosely at intervals. Wet thoroughly. Prepare the dyes according to manufacturer's instructions. Dye half the hank of string one color; rinse until water runs clear, then dye the other half in the second color. (If you want some natural string color to remain leave a gap between the two colors.) Rinse well and let dry.

For plant pot covers, unwind the hank and wind the string tightly around the plastic containers, fixing in place with clear glue.

For the desk 'tidy', first cut one of the tubes in half. Cut three circles from the cardboard and glue to the bottom of each tube. Then wind each tube with string, fixing it in place with clear glue. Glue the half tubes to the whole one as shown and tie in place until dry.

Découpage Boxes

Découpage is a fascinating craft which can be applied to all sorts of things. We've used it to decorate some empty chocolate boxes, but it can also be worked on trays, wooden boxes, tablemats and even furniture. Black is the best background color to accentuate the brightness of the cut-outs.

Materials
Chocolate boxes One 450g [1lb]; one 225g [½lb]
Cut-outs From magazines, posters, wrapping paper, transfer sheets (anything on thin paper)
Paint One standard tube black acrylic
Varnish 50ml [2fl oz] bottle, or plastic spray
Other items Paper paste

Apply two coats of black acrylic paint, drying between coats, to inside and outside of boxes.

Cut out shapes as required (we've used pretty flower shapes) with sharp scissors. Position them on the box lid to get a pleasing effect – put large shapes first, smaller ones on top. Glue in place. Glue more shapes around the sides, trimming away parts which go under closed lid. Leave to dry overnight.

Next day apply a coat of varnish or plastic spray inside and out. We filled the boxes with bought potpourri. *Note* For more durable découpage work on wood or tin apply anything up to 15–30 coats of varnish to get a completely smooth surface, with the cut-outs looking as though they are inlaid. Rub down between the last five coats with fine sandpaper wrapped around a sanding block. Keep on coating until the surface feels completely smooth, then rub down with extra fine sandpaper and apply a final coat of varnish.

For convenience, take a small can of varnish, punch a hole in the top and leave the brush in the varnish until the job is done.

57

Sewing

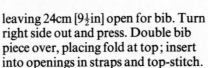

Unless otherwise stated, all patterns allow for 1.5cm [⅝in] seams.

Hostess Apron

So pretty – so practical: this long, ruffled apron protects a party dress from last-minute cooking spills.

Materials
Cotton 2m × 112cm [2¼yd × 44in]
Edging 7m × 6cm [7¾yd × 2⅜in] eyelet trim (broderie anglaise)

Size
Length from waist 89cm [35in]; straps adjustable

Cut fabric into these sizes:
Apron 91 × 86.5cm [36 × 34in]
Ties Two pieces 66 × 9cm [26 × 3½in]
Waistband Two pieces 66 × 7cm [26 × 2¾in]
Straps Four pieces 97 × 6cm [38 × 2⅜in]
Bib 48 × 20cm [19 × 8in]
Pocket 19 × 17cm [7½ × 6¾in]
(These sizes allow for 1cm [⅜in] seams)

Fold apron in half lengthwise and cut curve on lower corner. Repeat with pocket. Gather edging loosely and with right sides together sew around apron. Overcast raw edges; press edging outwards; push seam inwards and top-stitch in place.

Sew hem on pocket top; edge as for apron, folding 1.5cm [⅝in] over at top, and top-stitch to apron. Gather remaining edging; place inside straps and sew. Sew other edge of strap,

leaving 24cm [9½in] open for bib. Turn right side out and press. Double bib piece over, placing fold at top; insert into openings in straps and top-stitch.

Place bib piece inside waistband pieces; cross straps (adjust to fit here) and place inside band at ends leaving 1cm [⅜in] for seam. Stitch through all thicknesses. Fold ties in half lengthwise and sew. Turn right side out; place inside end of band and sew. Turn band right side out. Gather top edge of apron; stitch to back half of band. Turn under front band and top-stitch around all edges.

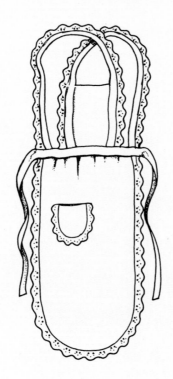

Play Wigwam

A wonderful toy for younger children, the colorful play wigwam can be put up indoors or out. To complete the picture make Indian headdresses: double bands of braid glued together, with some feathers in between at the front.

Materials

Canvas or sailcloth Two pieces in orange, 152.5 × 90cm [60 × 36in]; one piece in yellow, same size
Bamboo poles Five 2m [6ft] long
Webbing 7m × 4cm [7¾yd × 1½in]
Cotton tape 2m [2yd]
Fabric paint As desired
Meat skewers Four (for use as tent pegs)

Fold each piece of fabric in half lengthwise and mark center point at one end. Open out and draw lines from this point to opposite corners (diagram 1). Cut fabric on lines and down center to make four triangles from each piece; twelve in all (wigwam takes ten).

Join two triangles together down center; repeat to make two orange panels and two yellow ones. Then join all four together, with orange pair in center. Sew one orange triangle to each end, leaving last seam open for entrance at center front (diagram 2).

Pencil on Indian-style motifs and paint thickly with fabric paint.

Fold lower edge and hem. Trim off about 7.5cm [3in] at top edge; fold and top-stitch a seam to inside. Pin webbing to seam between each pair of triangles on the inside and stitch along each long edge leaving top and bottom ends open to insert bamboo poles.

Join center front seam for about 30cm [12in] from top. Hem front flap edges. Cut four lengths of tape 30cm [12in] long and attach to front flaps for ties.

Cut four lengths of tape 7cm [2¾in] long and sew double to center seam on each panel at lower edge to skewer wigwam to ground when erected.

Make a tie from surplus fabric about 50cm × 2.5cm [20 × 1in] to bind around top of bamboo poles.

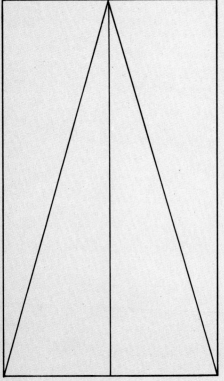

1

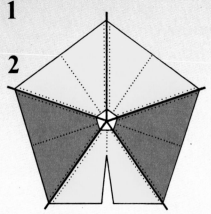

2

Simple Sam the Shepherd and His Lamb

Two soft toys to delight children and adults alike: Simple Sam the Shepherd and a newly arrived member of his flock.

Key

Felt A – brown hat (cut 1); B – black clog (cut 4); C – red mouth (cut 1); D – blue eye (cut 2); E – pink cheek (cut 2); F – pink nose (cut 1).
Smock G – back (cut 2); H – front, showing pleat line (cut 1); J yoke (cut 1); K – sleeve (cut 2); L – neck band (cut 1).
Trousers M – trousers (cut 4).
Doll N – head (cut 2); O – body (cut 2); P – leg (cut 4); Q – arm (cut 4).

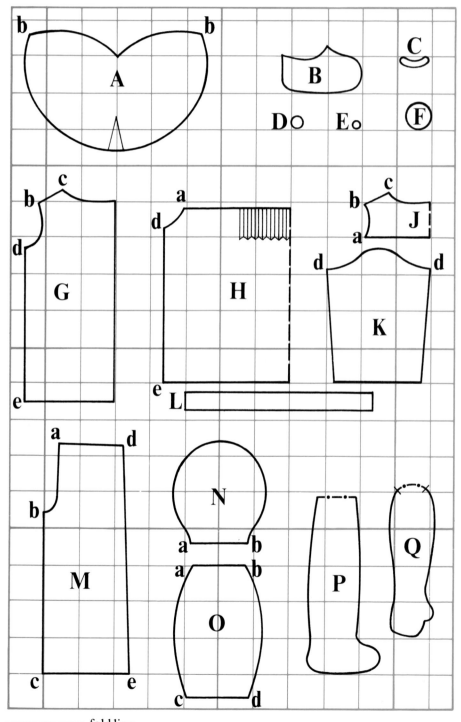

——— fold line
—·—·—·— opening

Simple Sam

Materials
Unbleached coarse muslin 50 × 90 or 112cm [18 × 36 or 44in]
Brown cotton 30 × 90 or 112cm [12 × 36 or 44in]
Blue cotton 50 × 90 or 112cm [18 × 36 or 44in]
Synthetic stuffing 500g [1lb]
Yellow yarn One small ball, for hair
Brown felt One piece 30cm [12in] square, for hat
Other items Scraps of pink, blue, red and black felt; brown yarn for eyebrows; scrap of polka dot fabric for kerchief; elastic and elastic thread; two snap (press-stud) fastenings; clear glue
Note In diagram, one square = 5cm [2in]

Size
50cm [20in] high

Scale up diagram on graph paper and cut out pieces. Use patterns to cut fabrics as indicated. (Pieces include a seam allowance of 6mm [¼in] unless otherwise stated.)

Doll Join each head piece to a body piece along a–b, then join front and back bodies from c around head to d. Join leg pieces together, then arms, leaving openings as indicated. Trim seams, turn pieces and stuff.

Insert leg tops in body opening c–d, fold in raw edges; top-stitch to close. Fold in raw edges of arms; close opening by top-stitching, then hand sew to body at sides below neck, thumbs facing front.

Glue on felt eyes, cheeks and mouth; embroider yarn eyebrows. Run a gathering thread around nose; draw up around some stuffing and sew on. Wind yarn for hair around a book. Tie

strands together at one edge and cut open at opposite edge. Sew knot to crown of head, arrange hair into a mop, stitch in place and trim to shape.

Trousers Join pieces together along a–b and open out; join front to back along each inside leg b–c and side d–e. Hem, and insert elastic at waist. Hand hem bottoms to fit doll; run elastic thread around each knee to gather.

Smock Open out front; run gathering threads across pleat lines and draw up to get accordion pleating so that a–a of front matches a–a of yoke. Then smock pleats.

Join front to yoke along a–a; join backs to front at shoulders b–c. Join each sleeve top to one open armhole from d, past a and b back to d. Join sleeve sides together from wrist to d. Join front to backs at sides from d to e.

Fold center back edges 2cm [¾in]; hem. Fold neck band in half lengthwise; fold under seam allowances; bind neck edge. Hem wrist and bottom edges to fit doll; close back with snap fasteners.

Clogs Join pieces leaving ankle edge free; trim and turn.

Hat and kerchief Join V-shaped edges from a to b; make dart; trim and turn. Cut polka dot fabric into a triangle and hem.

Little Lamb

Materials
White fur fabric 80 × 75cm [32 × 30in]
Brown fur fabric 10 × 20cm [4 × 8in]
Synthetic stuffing 500g [1lb]
Other items Scraps of brown felt; two black buttons for eyes
Note In diagram, one square = 5cm [2in]

Size
38cm [15in] high × 40cm [16in] long

Scale up diagram on graph paper and cut out. Use patterns to cut out fabrics as indicated, making sure that pile of fur fabric always runs towards rear of animal. (Pieces include a seam allowance of 6mm [¼in] unless otherwise stated.)

Join muzzle to head gusset along a–a to get one head top. Join a side muzzle to each body piece along a–b

to complete body outline. Join each inside leg gusset to one body piece from b round legs to c, leaving openings at feet for soles, as indicated on diagram.

Join an edge of head top to each body along d–a–e, then join bodies between c–d and e–b; finally join leg gussets from b to c, leaving an opening for stuffing. Trim seams; turn right side out and stuff firmly.

Hand stitch leg gusset opening. Fold in fur edges at feet, and edges of felt soles; firmly hand stitch one sole to each foot.

With right sides together, join ear pieces from x to y, leaving open an edge as indicated on diagram. Trim, turn and hand stitch one to each side of head.

Fold tail in two, curved edge and right sides facing, and stitch along curved seam. Turn and sew open end to body at c with seam on underside.

Sew on eyes as in picture; tease out fur pile from the seams.

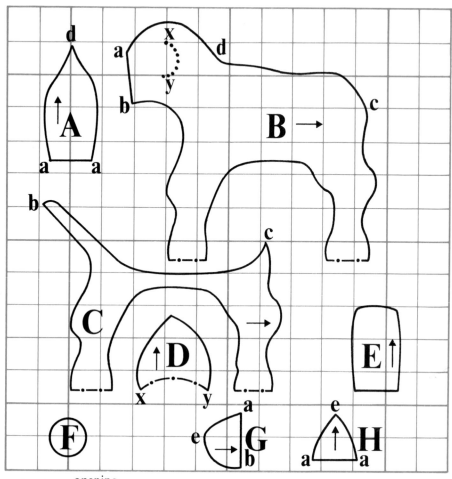

Key
Arrow shows direction of fur fabric pile.
White fur A – head gusset (cut 1); B – body (cut 2); C – inside leg gusset (cut 2); D – ear (cut 4); E – tail (cut 1).
Brown felt F – sole (cut 4).
Brown fur G – side muzzle (cut 2); H – muzzle (cut 1).

—.—.— opening
••••••••• sewing

Toddlers' Play Clothes

The little girls' pinafore and dungarees may look charming, but they're tough enough to stand up to the rough and tumble of play. And if they're filthy at the end of the day, toss them in the washing machine and they'll come out smiling time after time.

Dungarees

Materials
Corduroy 1m × 112cm [1⅛yd × 44in]
Felt Scrap for design if desired
Other items 35 × 2.5cm [14 × 1in] tape; 30 × 12mm [12 × ½in] elastic; two buttons
Note In diagram, one square = 5cm [2in]

Sizes
To fit 1½- to 2-year-old and 2- to 3-year-old

Scale up diagram on graph paper and cut out pieces. Pin to fabric and cut out number indicated. Also cut a piece 14 × 15cm [5½ × 6in] for pocket.

If desired, apply design to pocket. (There is a teddy bear design on page 145; enlarge him to 10cm [4in] high, cut out in felt and appliqué to fabric with close zigzag stitch.)

Sew fronts to backs at side seams and inner leg seams. Turn one leg right side out and place inside other leg so that right sides are together. Sew crotch seam.

Join strap pieces together, leaving straight ends open. Turn right side out and top-stitch straps. Pin to back

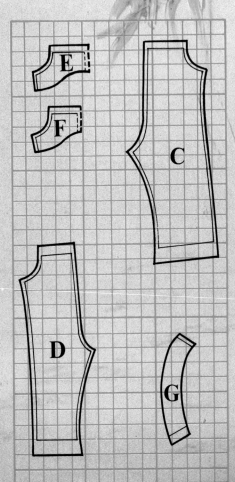

Sizes:
——— 1½–2 years
━━━ 2–3 years
----- fold line

66

ensuring that they curve out towards side seams.

Hem ends of tape and sew to inside back of waist on long edges only. Insert elastic; adjust to fit, and stitch firmly at both ends to make gathering.

Fold under top pocket edge 4cm [1½in] and hem. Fold in remaining 1cm [⅜in] seam allowance; place pocket on center front and stitch in place.

Stitch facings together at side seams. Sew to body, right sides together, with straps in seam. Turn facing to inside and tack to side seams.

Make buttonhole each side of top front. Sew buttons to straps. Fold under lower edge of legs and hem.

Pinafore

Materials
Patterned cotton 60 × 90 or 112cm [24 × 36 or 44in]
Bias binding 5m [5½yd]
Note In diagram, one square = 5cm [2in]

Size
To fit a 2- to 3-year-old.

Scale up diagram on graph paper and cut out pieces. Pin on to fabric and cut one front with center on fold; two backs, and two pockets.

Round off lower corner of back pieces into an even curve. Edge pockets with bias binding and sew to front piece. Join shoulder and side seams. Bind armholes. Starting at neck edge bind all around back edges and lower edge of pinafore. Leaving 25cm [10in] of binding free for ties at each end, bind neck edge. Fold neck ties in half lengthwise and sew. Cut two pieces of binding 25cm [10in] long, fold in half lengthwise and sew, then stitch to back edges 14cm [5½in] down from neck ties.

Key
Pinafore A – front (cut 1) and back (cut 2); B – pocket (cut 2).
Dungarees C – back (cut 2); D – front (cut 2); E – back facing (cut 1); F – front facing (cut 1); G – strap (cut 4).

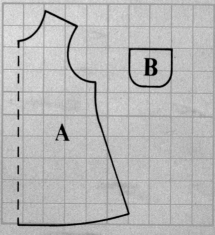

Bath Robe

This wrap-around robe couldn't be easier to make: only the back and fronts need a pattern; all other pieces are rectangles of various sizes. Terry toweling is the obvious choice for a beach or bath robe, but you could successfully use printed fine corduroy for a feminine housecoat; lightweight polyester for a man's travel robe; pre-quilted cotton for warmth; or patterned black satin for the Oriental look.

Materials

Terry toweling 4.2m × 90cm [4½yd × 36in] for medium size; 4.6m × 90cm [5yd × 36in] for large size
Note In diagram, one square = 5cm [2in]

Sizes

Medium size fits 92–97cm [36–38in]
Large size fits 107–112cm [42–44in] chest

Scale up diagram pattern for back and fronts on graph paper. Use to cut out fabric, placing center back of pattern on fold.
Then cut out the following pieces:

Medium size
Sleeve Two pieces 63.5 × 53.5cm [25 × 21in]
Band Two pieces 127 × 14cm [50 × 5½in]
Belt Two pieces 89 × 13cm [35 × 5¼in]

Large size
Sleeves Two pieces 63.5 × 63.5cm [25 × 25in]
Band Two pieces 140 × 14cm [55 × 5½in]
Belt Two pieces 119 × 13cm [47 × 5¼in]

Both sizes
Pockets Two pieces 24 × 22cm [9½ × 8¾in]
Belt carriers Two pieces 10 × 3cm [4 × 1¼in]

Fold over 4cm [1½in] hem on pocket tops and stitch. Press seams under and top-stitch to robe fronts 5cm [2in] in from side seam, with bottom about 50cm [20in] up.
Stitch front to back at shoulders. Align center sleeve top with shoulder seam; stitch sleeve to body. Join sleeve and side seams. Clip seam at armhole. Fold under 18.5cm [7¼in] for cuff; hem in place.

Fold under lower hem of robe and stitch. Join band pieces together at back neck. Align right side of band with inside edge of robe; stitch to fronts and around back neck. Press seam flat; double band over, folding seam allowance under, and top-stitch to robe. Fold under lower edge of band and tack in place.

Join belt pieces at center back. Fold in half lengthwise, stitch ends and length, leaving 15cm [6in] open at center back. Turn right side out and close opening.

Fold under edges of belt carriers and stitch. Attach to side seams firmly.

Key

A – back (cut 1); B – front (cut 2).

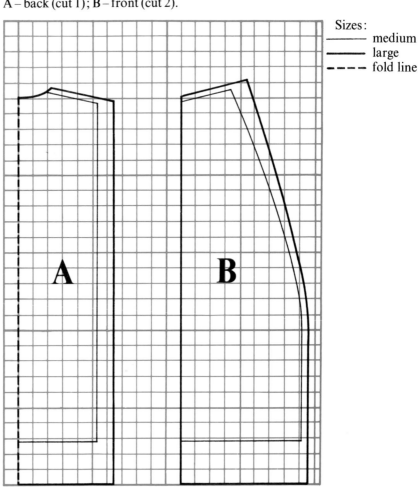

Sizes:
———— medium
——— large
- - - - fold line

Mrs. Mouse Quilt

Here is an enchanting appliqué quilt, sized to fit a crib or baby carriage.

Materials

White cotton One piece 69 × 89cm [27 × 35in] for backing; one piece 43 × 63cm [17 × 25in] for center
Blue cotton Two pieces 15 × 89cm [6 × 35in]; two pieces 15 × 63cm [6 × 25in] for borders
Padding One piece 90 × 70cm [36 × 27in]
Other items Scraps of cottons and felt for appliqué; dark brown embroidery thread; 50cm [18in] eyelet trim (broderie anglaise)
Note In diagram, one square = 10cm [4in]

Scale up the diagram on graph paper. With tracing paper make a pattern of each shape, allowing 1cm [⅜in] extra where shapes meet to overlap for strength. Cut out in fabric and felt.

Arrange picture on center piece of quilt, pin and baste in place. With close zigzag machine edges of shapes to quilt, setting in eyelet trim on lower edge of dress and at cuffs. Embroider eyes, whiskers and broom.

Sew borders to quilt center leaving ends loose. Miter at corners and sew. Sew backing to quilt, leaving opening at lower edge. Insert padding, close opening. Machine stitch through all thicknesses around inside border edge.

Baby's Sleeping Bag

A cozy, fleecy sleeping bag for a small baby, this pretty and practical gift unbuttons at the bottom to become a dressing gown later on.

Materials

Acrylic fleece 180 × 122cm [2yd × 48in]
Other items 46cm [18in] open-end zipper; seven buttons
Note In diagram, one square = 5cm [2in]

Size

To fit 6- to 12-month-old baby

Scale up the diagram on graph paper and cut out the pieces. Pin on to fabric and cut one body, two sleeves and two collars. Also cut one piece 49 × 43cm [19¼ × 17in] for lower bag.

Stitch dart at top of sleeves. Join sleeve seam. With right sides together sew raglan sleeve into armhole of body. Fold under 3cm [1¼in] at front edges for facings.

Stitch outer edge of collar pieces with right sides together and turn right side out. Place right side of collar on inside of body; stitch collar to neck. Hem under-collar to back neck. Top-stitch collar.

Fold up sleeves 2.5cm [1in] and hem. Insert zipper in fronts. Fold up hem 5cm [2in] and stitch in herringbone.

Fold bag piece in half, inside out, and join side seams. Fold under 4cm [1½in] around top and stitch in place. Make three buttonholes in front top hem and four in back. Sew buttons on body piece to correspond.

Key
A – sleeve (cut 2); B – collar (cut 2);
C – body (cut 1).

Patchwork Cozies and Chair Pillow

As the patches are all machine-stitched, both cozies and pillow are quick to make. The pillow is very economical as it uses up triangles left over from making a cozy. The cozies are designed to fit a standard-size tea or coffee pot.

Tea Cozy

Materials
Cotton Eight squares in different patterns, 23 × 23cm [9 × 9in]; one strip for ruffle 100 × 6cm [39 × 2½in]; two strips for lower border 35 × 6cm [14 × 2½in]
Padding Two pieces 35 × 25cm [14 × 10in]
Lining One piece of cotton 30 × 90cm [12 × 36in]
Note In diagram, one square = 5cm [2in]

Cut each square into four, then each small square diagonally across making eight triangles. Arrange triangles on a flat surface, alternating light and dark colors as shown. Each side takes twenty-two triangles. Machine stitch two triangles together diagonally, with 1cm [⅜in] seams; repeat until you have made ten squares. Keeping arrangement even, stitch four squares together to form a strip. Repeat and join two strips together. Sew top triangles to last two squares and join to rest of cozy piece. Sew on lower border strip. Repeat to make two sides.

Make a paper pattern to the shape shown in diagram, 25cm high × 35cm wide [10 × 14in]. Pin to patchwork pieces, lower edge to bottom of border; cut surplus away. Use same pattern to cut lining and padding. Fold and gather ruffle to fit around cozy. With right sides together, ruffle sandwiched between two halves, stitch around top edge of cozy, ending ruffle about 1.5cm [⅝in] from lower edge.

Sew lining pieces together, leaving about 20cm [8in] open at the top. Place over cozy, right sides together, and sew to lower edge. Sew padding pieces together and place inside cozy. Fold lining inside and close opening.

Coffee Cozy
The pattern for this should be the same shape as for the tea cozy, but 10cm [4in] higher and 5cm [2in] narrower. It will take thirty-six triangles.

Pillow

Materials
Cotton One piece 70 × 90cm [27 × 36in]; sixteen small triangles left over from cozy
Pillow form 40cm [16in] square

Cut three strips 6cm [2½in] wide across width of fabric for ruffle. Cut four strips 44 × 10cm [17½ × 4in] from length for front borders. Arrange triangles on a flat surface, alternating light and dark colors as shown to form a square. Stitch together allowing 1cm [⅜in] seams.

Fold border strips in half and mark center. With right sides together, place center mark of border at center of edge of patchwork square. Stitch, leaving ends free. Miter corners of border and stitch. Trim surplus material, press seams open.

Cut a backing square from remaining fabric, using front as a pattern. Join ruffle strips together; fold and gather to fit round pillow. Stitch two right sides of pillow together, sandwiching ruffle into seam and leaving about 20cm [8in] open on one side. Turn right sides out and sew ruffle to front of pillow at opening. Insert pillow form and close opening with stitching or a zipper.

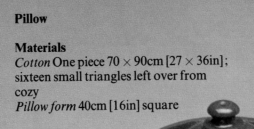

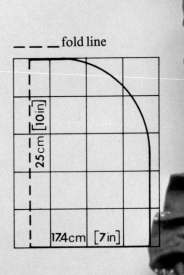

_ _ _ _ fold line

10in
25cm
17·4cm [7in]

Tool Hanger

Materials
Canvas or sailcloth 1.2m × 90 or 112cm
[1⅜yd × 36 or 44in]
Dowel rod Two pieces 74 × 1.2cm
diam. [29 × ½in diam.]
Strong nylon cord 1m [1yd]
For decoration 2m × 2.5cm [2yd × 1in]
braid; twenty rivets

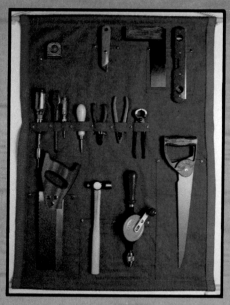

Cut fabric for base 70 × 100cm
[27 × 40in]. Cut a piece of paper the
same size and on it lay out the tools
to be accommodated, placing the
heaviest at the bottom. With pencil,
draw patterns for the pockets to fit
loosely around each tool. Allow for a
row of loops to take small tools; you
could also add extra pockets for items
like sandpaper, packs of nails and
screws, etc.

Cut pockets from remaining fabric to
desired size, adding 3cm [1¼in] for
seams on each piece. Fold in seam
allowance on pocket pieces and hem
pocket tops.

Fold seam allowance on side edges to
right side and top-stitch braid in place
down each edge. Arrange pockets as
desired and sew firmly in place. Make
a hem 4cm [1½in] deep at the top and
bottom of hanger leaving ends open,
and insert dowels.

Reinforce pocket tops with rivets at
corners. Drill a hole in each end of top
dowel and knot nylon cord through.

Designed to hold a basic tool kit, this
useful hanger can be carried from the
workshop or garage and hung on a hook
or door handle wherever the actual
job is to be done. In this way it serves
two purposes: as well as keeping all the
tools together ready for use, it cuts out
the usual running back and forth to
fetch tools that didn't at first appear to
be needed. The idea can also be adapted
to make a hanger for sewing clutter or
children's toys.

Shopping Bags

A colorful canvas shopping bag, personalized with the recipient's initials or a fun motif, makes a present that will be in use for a long time.

Materials
Canvas or sailcloth 80 × 122cm [32 × 48in]
Cotton or felt Scrap(s) for motif

Cut canvas into following pieces:
Bag Two pieces 50 × 50cm [19¾ × 19¾in]
Handles Two pieces 122 × 10cm [48 × 4in] for long handles; or two pieces 46 × 10cm [18 × 4in] for short handles.

Cut out an 8 × 8cm [3⅛ × 3⅛in] square from lower corners of bag pieces. Make up desired motif (see pages 144–9) and apply to one piece. Sew pieces together at base seam.

For long handles, fold pieces in half lengthwise, inside out; stitch and turn out. Join ends to form a circle. Sew handles to bag, about 12.5cm [5in] apart, placing joining seam at base seam of bag, and leaving 5cm [2in] free at top edge for seams.

Join side seams. Place side seam to base seam and close lower opening. Fold under top edge and sew, leaving handles free. Pull up handles and sew to top edge of bag firmly.

For short handles, join lengthwise, turn out and attach firmly to top hem inside bag.

To emphasize bag shape, top-stitch close to edge on all four sides, starting at bottom corner and running parallel to long handles or side seams.

Hobby Smocks

His-and-hers smocks are based on the traditional sailing jackets worn by fishermen. They are perfect for any kind of hobby, whether it's sewing or carpentry, painting or gardening, as well as sailing. The loose fit makes them very comfortable and ample pockets keep small tools and odds and ends ready for instant use.

Materials
Denim, sailcloth, etc. 1.7m × 142cm [1⅞yd × 56in] for medium size; 2.2m [2½yd] for large size
Note In diagram, one square = 5cm [2in]

Sizes
Actual chest/bust measurements 104cm [41in] and 119cm [47in]

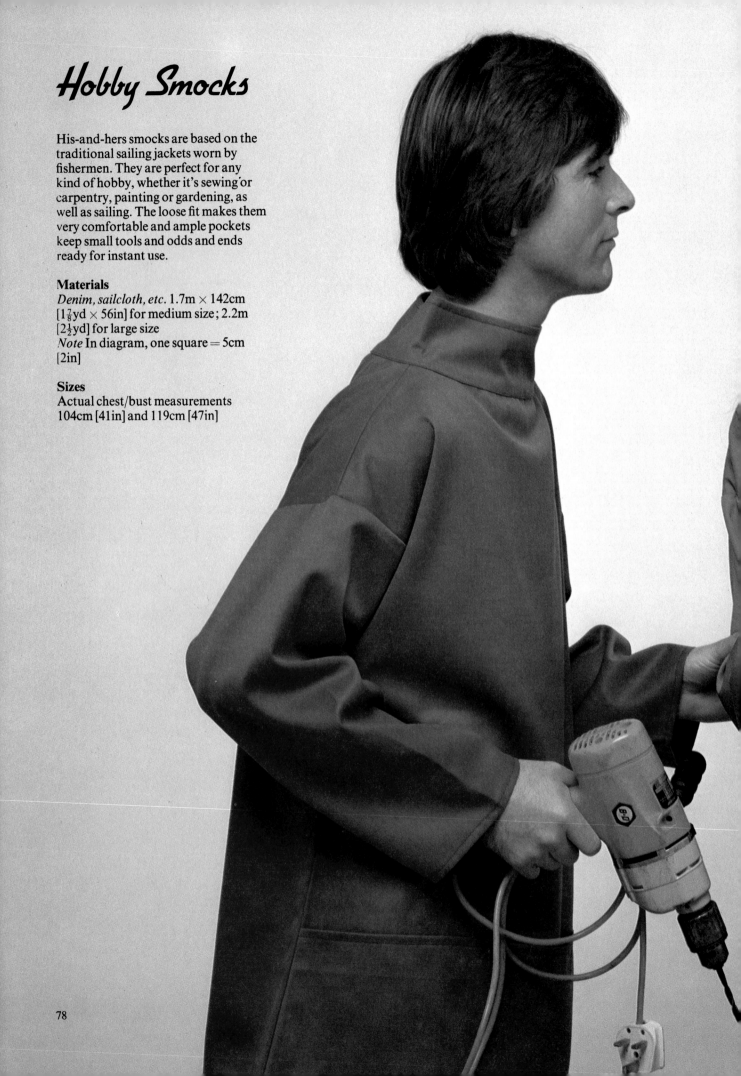

Scale up diagram on graph paper and cut out pieces, placing on fold of material where indicated.

Hem top edge of pocket; fold seams under; place pocket on front and stitch in place. Divide into three, with a double line of top-stitching.

Join back and front at shoulders.

Join collar pieces at center back of neck. Right sides together, join collar pieces together along top edge; turn right side out. Match seam to center back, sew inside of collar around neck. Push seam upwards; bring outside collar over seam; turn under seam allowance and top-stitch. Top-stitch top edge.

Sew sleeves into armhole. Join side and underarm seams. Fold up hem at lower edge and at cuffs and top-stitch.

Key
A – front (cut 1) and back (cut 1);
B – collar (cut 2); C – sleeve (cut 2);
D – pocket (cut 1).

Sizes:
_____ medium   _ _ _. fold line
_____ large   .... sewing line

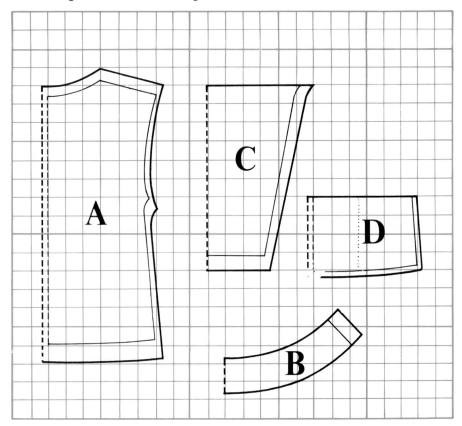

Cosmetic Bag

This pretty little quilted bag couldn't be simpler to make. To turn it into a sponge bag, replace the inner layer of fabric with plastic.

Materials
Cotton Two pieces 40 × 20cm
[16 × 8in]
Padding One piece 40 × 20cm
[16 × 8in]
Other items 1m [1yd] binding; large snap (press stud) fastening

Place the two pieces of fabric together, right sides out; fold in half lengthwise and cut curve around one end for flap. Place padding in between the two pieces and pin together firmly. Draw chalk or pencil lines for quilting, using both sides of a ruler – this automatically gives you parallel lines. Baste and stitch through all thicknesses. Cut away surplus padding. Bind straight end. Fold over 12.5cm [5in] and sew sides. Trim seam and bind all around edge. Apply large snap fastening to center flap and bag.

Clothespin Bag

This easy-to-make clothespin bag is mounted on a cut-down clothes hanger so it hangs on the washing line

Materials
Patterned cotton Two pieces 35.5 × 33cm [14 × 13in]
Plain cotton Two pieces same size for lining
Other items Wooden clothes hanger

Fold one piece of patterned fabric in half lengthwise. Mark a point 15cm [6in] down from unfolded top corner, and 7.5cm [3in] from corner along top edge. Pencil a line from point to point and cut off the triangle. This forms the back. For the front, mark same points but cut a curved line – see photograph.

Use these two pieces as a pattern to cut two identical pieces in lining.

Join lining pieces at top edge. Join outside pieces at top edge, leaving a small gap in center for the hook of the hanger. Place lining and outside pieces together, right sides facing, and sew all around pocket edges; clip curve and turn right side out. Join side edges of outside and lining separately. Sew lower edge of lining. Cut hanger to fit top and place between lining and outside, inserting hook through top seam. Turn under lower edge and top-stitch.

Oven Mitts

The bold check fabric used for quilted oven mitts makes them so easy to quilt: the lines follow the checks, either up and down or diagonally, as you please.

Materials (for one)
Cotton Two pieces 70 × 20cm [27½ × 8in]; four pieces 18 × 20cm [7 × 8in]
Padding One piece 70 × 20cm [27½ × 8in]; two pieces 18 × 20cm [7 × 8in]
Binding 2m [2¼yd]

Place padding between the pieces of cotton, right sides out, and pin together firmly. With chalk or pencil, draw quilting lines, using the checks as a grid. Baste and stitch through all thicknesses.

Round off corners at ends of long strip and hand pieces. Sew hand pieces to strip, trim surplus and bind all around edge.

Barbecue Apron

Solve the 'what-on-earth-can-I-give-*him*?' problem with our simple apron pattern. We've made it up with matching mitt for a barbecue enthusiast, but it can be endlessly varied. Make it in butcher's striped fabric for a keen cook, or in plain fabric for a Sunday painter or dedicated carpenter, all with suitable inscriptions. If inspiration fails, decorate with his name, or a motif – see pages 144–9.

Apron

Materials

Blue denim 90cm × 1.5m [1 × 1½yd]
Tape 2m × 1.2cm [2yd × ½in]
Fabric paints As desired
Note In diagram, one square = 5cm [2in]

Size

The pattern suits a tall man – for a shorter one simply reduce length of strap.

Scale up diagram on graph paper and cut out pieces; pin on to fabric and cut out. Also cut one piece 36 × 24cm [14½ × 9½in] for pocket and one piece 32 × 7.5cm [12½ × 3in] for apron top facing.

Paint design on front.

Hem one long edge of pocket; fold remaining edges under and top-stitch pocket to apron. Divide in center with a line of stitching.

Join neck pieces at center back; fold seam allowance under along long edges, and top-stitch together to make neck strap. Pin strap to right side of apron top at each side, leaving 1.5cm [⅝in] at edges for seams.

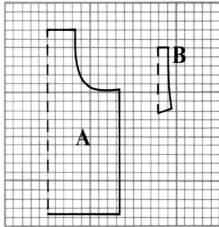

— — — fold line

A – apron (cut 1); B – neck band (cut 2).

Hem one long edge (to be bottom edge) of facing. Place facing over straps and apron top, and sew together through all thicknesses. Fold so that facing is inside and straps are flat with apron top.

Fold remaining seam and hem allowance and machine stitch around entire edge of apron including top edge.

Cut tape in two lengths of 76cm [30in] and sew on to apron for ties.

Mitt

Materials

Blue denim or scraps
Padding 50cm [18in]
Bias binding 2m × 2.5cm [2yd × 1in]

Draw a pattern around hand (with fingers slightly splayed) for required size. Cut four pieces of denim and two pieces of padding. Place padding between each pair of denim pieces and quilt together. Sew mitt pieces together on right side; trim surplus fabric. Bind wrist edge. Bind around hand, leaving enough binding at outside edge to turn back for loop.

Windmill Play Quilt

This quilt has a story hidden in it: whatever story you care to make up, moving the mice and sacks of flour around the landscape in the pockets provided. When not in use on a child's bed, it can be hung on the wall.

Materials

Cotton One piece 1.5m × 112cm [60 × 44in] for backing

Brushed denim Two pieces 145 × 16.5cm [57 × 6½in]; two pieces 99 × 16.5cm [39 × 6½in] for borders; blue and green for background

Padding One piece 94 × 140cm [37 × 55in]

Brown ribbon 1·4m × 1cm [55 × ⅜in] for windmill sails

Other items Scraps of cottons, linen, felt, corduroy, etc for appliqué and clothes for mice; small pieces of felt and trimmings; one wooden bead for door; thin cord for boat mooring; cotton (cotton wool) to stuff sacks; snap (press stud) fastenings; 1m × 2.5cm [1yd × 1in] tape; 1m × 1.2cm [1yd × ½in] dowel rod; pipe cleaners; brown felt

Note In diagram 1, one square = 10cm [4in]

Finished size

94 × 140cm [37 × 55in]

Scale up diagram 1 on graph paper. Trace appliqué shapes, allowing 1cm [⅜in] extra where shapes overlap, and for pockets. Cut out of desired fabrics. (On shapes with pockets, sew along pocket edge and trim before placing on quilt.) Cut out background and join together at skyline with close zigzag stitch. Sew ribbon for back of sails, pencil in rest of sail and machine embroider. Arrange picture on quilt; pin and baste in place. Sew to background with close zigzag, leaving pockets open. Machine stitch on details and trimmings.

Sew borders to picture, leaving ends open. Miter ends and sew together. If quilt is to hang up on wall, sew tape to top of backing to take dowel rod. Sew backing to quilt, leaving opening at lower edge. Insert padding and close opening. Sew through all thicknesses around inside edge of border, around

84

windmill shape, and path.

Make three small sacks; stuff them, and fasten to quilt with snap (press stud) fastenings.

Mouse (make three)

Twist four pipe cleaners together as in diagram 2. Make head in felt, place over pipe cleaner and stuff. Sew on ears and features. Cut strips of felt for arms and legs. Sew one end and long edge; slip on pipe cleaner and glue in place. Cover top of body with cotton for shirt and make trousers in felt. Sew strip of felt for tail and sew in place.

Key
All mouse pattern pieces are actual size. A – head (cut 2); B – head gusset (cut 1); C – ear (cut 2).

openings for pockets –·–·–·–

Small Presents

Scented Things

Up-dated versions of the lavender bags great-grandmother used to put in her linen closet are quick and easy to sew and make charming small presents. Make little sachets for use in drawers; hanging ones for clothes closets (include a matching coat hanger to make a bigger present); herb pillows for poor sleepers. The pomanders are a different way of capturing a delicious spicy scent, and the giant mouse, stuffed with catnip, is a present for the family cat. You can buy dried flowers and herbs from health food stores and herb specialists; or make your own filling with the instructions below. The fabric used for sachets should be lightweight and closely woven.

Potpourri

Any scented flowers or leaves can be used for potpourri. Rose and lavender are the most popular, but other good ones are rosemary flowers and leaves; rose geranium leaves, and carnations. Spices are also added, and these can be varied to taste; plus a fixative, often ground orrisroot.

Pick the flowers early on a dry day; pluck off the petals, and spread out on a tray. Leave in a moderately warm place, turning each day, for about five days, until they are like tissue paper.

For rose potpourri: to every four large handfuls of dried petals add 50g [2oz] each of ground orrisroot and coriander, and four teaspoons ground cinnamon. Put into a jar with a lid; shake well together, and leave for 2–3 weeks, shaking or stirring frequently.

For traditional lavender bags, use the dried flowers alone. For a more subtle scent mix 225g [8oz] dried lavender flowers with four teaspoons each of dried thyme and mint, one tablespoon table salt, and two teaspoons each of ground cloves and caraway seeds.

Hanging Hearts

Materials
Red fabric Scraps
White ribbon 70 × 1cm [¾yd × ⅜in]
Filling Cotton (cotton wool); potpourri

Use pattern to cut six heart shapes, adding 1cm [½in] seam allowance all around. Place together in pairs, right sides facing, and stitch, leaving a small opening. Trim seam and turn right side out. Fill with potpourri and a little cotton (cotton wool). Close opening.

Fold ribbon in half. Leaving a 5cm [2in] loop at the top, center hearts on folded ribbon, leaving 2.5cm [1in] space between each one, and stitch along the back. Cut ends of ribbon into V-shapes.

Lavender Bags

Materials (for one)
Print fabric 18 × 10cm [7 × 4in]
Lace trimming 25 × 1cm [10 × ⅜in]
Braided cord (for hanging) 18cm [7in]
Filling Lavender or desired mixture

Cut two circles from fabric, 8.5cm [3¼in] diam. Baste lace trimming around right side of one, 1cm [⅜in] in from edge, facing towards center. Place second circle on top and stitch, leaving small opening. Trim seams and turn right side out. Fill with lavender. Close opening, catching in braid folded in half, if bag is to hang up.

Covered Coat Hanger

Materials
Fabric (to match bag) 50 × 50cm [20 × 20in]
Other items Wooden coat hanger; cotton (cotton wool); clear glue; 1m [1yd] narrow ribbon

Cover cotton (cotton wool) over both sides of coat hanger and secure by winding around with thread. Wind ribbon around the hook, starting at top and finishing with a few stitches at base.

Place hanger on the bias (slanting) on wrong side of fabric; draw around at

hook side and ends but not at base. Turn hanger over and mark second side, to make one pattern piece. Cut out, adding 1cm [⅜in] seam allowance. Fold fabric upwards over hanger; fold in seam allowance at ends and top and slip-stitch together. (If hanger is very curved, you may have a little too much fabric at top; simply trim away.) Tie ribbon bow around base of hook.

Flying Bird

Materials
Print fabric 32 × 32cm [12½ × 12½in]
Other items Scrap red felt; braided cord; two tiny red beads; clear glue
Filling Cotton (cotton wool); lavender

Use pattern to cut out two birds and four wings, adding 1cm [⅜in] seam allowance all around. Cut two felt triangles for beak.

Place bird pieces with right sides together and stitch, leaving an opening at back and two small openings at a and b for beak and hanging cord. Trim seam and turn right side out. Stuff bird and close back opening.

Stick beak triangles together; put into beak opening, and slip-stitch in place at a. Fold hanging cord in half and slip-stitch in place at b.

On right side of two wing pieces (make sure to make a pair), top-stitch two rows of stitching all around. Place plain and stitched wing pieces with right sides together in pairs and stitch, leaving an opening. Trim seam and turn right side out. Fill bird with cotton wool and lavender; sew opening closed.

Sew wings to each side of body and beads for eyes on head.

Giant Mouse

Materials
Print fabric 36 × 20cm [14 × 8in]
Other items Scrap of white felt; white yarn; two white beads; white button thread
Filling Catnip and a little stuffing

Scale up the diagram on graph paper, adding 1cm [⅜in] seam allowance all around. Use to cut two bodies and one base in print fabric; two ears in felt.

Stitch bodies together along top seam; stitch base into opening, leaving a gap. Trim seams and turn right side out. Fill with catnip and a little stuffing; sew opening closed.

Sew ears each side of head, making a small tuck in the base. Sew on bead

eyes. Braid three lengths of yarn for tail and sew to rear. Make a few whiskers with button thread.
Note If you cannot obtain dried catnip, you could find it in someone's garden – catmint (Nepeta cataria). Dry as described for potpourri.

Herb Pillow

Materials
Print fabric 30 × 90cm [12 × 36in]
Lace 140 × 4.5cm [1½yd × 1¾in]
Filling 30 × 90cm [12 × 36in] cotton padding; aromatic herbs

Cut fabric into two pieces 30 × 45cm [12 × 18in]. Tack lace all around right side of one piece, 2cm [¾in] from edges, mitering the corners. Hand sew neatly in place.

Place fabric pieces right sides together; stitch (with 1cm [⅜in] seam), leaving an opening at one side. Trim seam, cutting diagonally across corners. Turn right side out.

Cut two pieces of padding to fit inside pillow. Spread the dried herbs between the two pieces and place inside pillow. Fold in seam allowance on open edges and slip-stitch together.

Pomander

Materials
One orange; whole cloves; ground cinnamon and orrisroot; waxed (greaseproof) paper; ribbon or cord

The traditional method is to stick the orange as full of cloves as possible, but this is not essential and we only used about 25g [1oz] for each orange, arranging them in various patterns. As a guide you can bind the orange with thread to mark it into sections. If the cloves are very brittle, prick the orange with a fine needle to help get them in.

Roll the orange in a mixture of equal parts of ground cinnamon and orrisroot, rubbing in well. Wrap in waxed (greaseproof) paper and put away for 5–6 weeks for the aroma to develop and the orange to shrivel. Tie around with ribbon or cord, putting a loop at the top for hanging.

Key
All pattern pieces are actual size.
Hanging heart A – heart (cut 6).
Flying bird B – body (cut 2); C – wing (cut 2).
Giant mouse D – body (cut 2); E – ear (cut 2); F – base (cut 1).

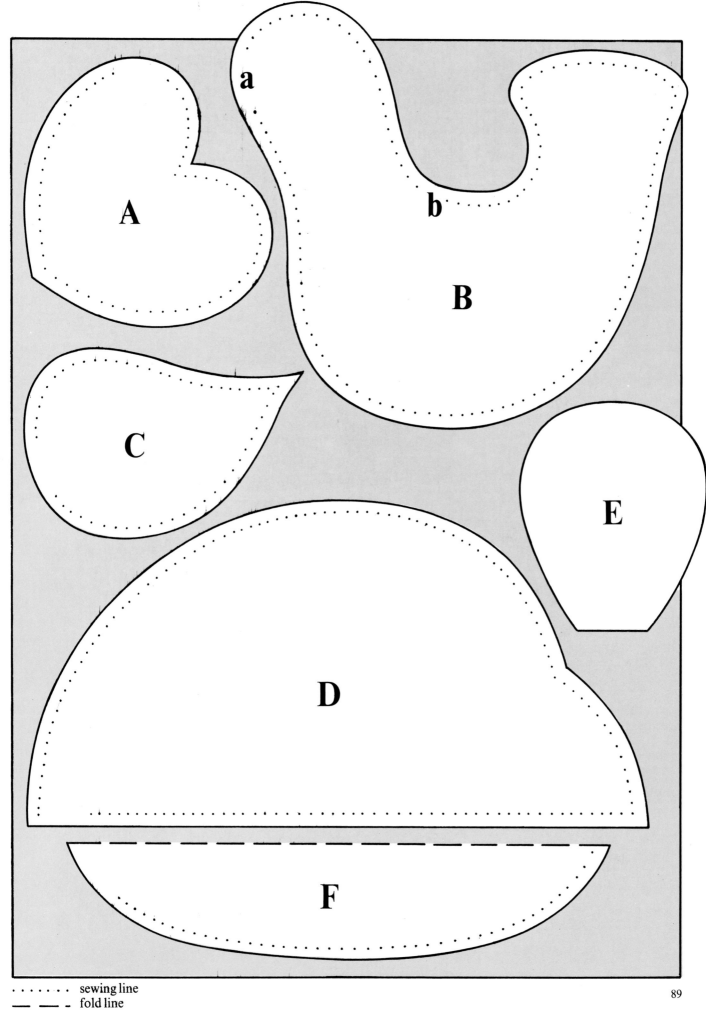

A

a

b

B

C

E

D

F

· · · · · · · sewing line
— — — fold line

Painted Stones

Stones from the seashore are beautifully smooth and often interestingly shaped by wave action. Attractively decorated, they can become paperweights, door stops, or just ornaments. The ones shown in the picture were all painted by children under ten years old.

Materials
Stones; poster paints, poster varnish

Wash the stones and let dry thoroughly. Paint one side as desired; if you don't want to paint freehand, you can copy one of the motifs on pages 144–9.
 Let dry and paint second side; (all the animal stones in the photograph have got a back view on the reverse side). Finish with poster varnish.

Shell Animals
Common-or-garden sea shells gathered from the beach can be used to make delightful little animals. We've made a snail, a tortoise, a dachshund, a hedgehog or porcupine, a frog and a trio of mice; but the trick is to make whatever suggests itself from the shells you happen to have.

Materials
Assorted small sea shells; epoxy resin adhesive; varnish; leftover enamel paint; thin cardboard

Wash the shells and leave overnight in in a warm place so that they dry thoroughly inside as well as out.
 Sort out appropriate shells to make an animal, and decide which is going where. Mix up the epoxy resin adhesive according to the instructions (you don't have long to work with this type, but it is very strong). Glue the shells together, and leave to dry overnight. Test the strength of the adhesive bonds and if some shells have not stuck firmly, scrape the glue off and re-glue. When dry, varnish with whatever you have on hand – clear nail polish does perfectly well.
 Paint in features such as the tortoise's shell before varnishing, but add paper parts like the frog's feet last of all.

Knitted Dolls

Snowman and Santa Claus, pirate and soldier, baby and clown – these are only a few of the enchanting little figures you can make from this pattern just by changing the color of the yarn and varying the features and accessories.

Materials
Scraps of knitting worsted (double knitting) yarn
3¼mm [No. 3] knitting needles
Felt, wooden beads, material scraps, clear glue, stuffing

Size
About 16.5cm [6½in] high

Legs (make two)
Cast on 13 sts and work 4cm [1½in] in st st.

Body
Work across both sets sts from legs for 2.5cm [1in] to waist. Change color here if desired. Work a further 4cm [1½in] to shoulder.

Neck
K1 * K2 tog., K1; rep. from * to end.
P 1 row. Change color for face.

Face
K1 * inc. 1, K1; rep. from * to end.
Work 2.5cm [1in] st st for face; change color and work about the same amount for hair or hat.
Next row K2 tog all across row. P1 row.
Next row K2 tog to last st, K1. Thread yarn through sts and draw up.

Arms (make two)
Cast on 9 sts and work 1.2cm [½in] st st for hand. Work 5cm [2in] for arm. K2 tog across row. Draw up sts.

Finishing
Join leg seams. Join center back, inserting stuffing before completing. Sew up arms; stuff and sew to body. Run a gathering thread through neck and wrists and draw up to shape them.
    Add felt features and accessories as desired.

Felt Menagerie

All you need to make these colorful animals are scraps of felt and a few odds and ends. The patterns given make an owl, a parrot, a snake and a short-legged bird of unknown breed; but once you've made one or two you'll find it easy to make your own patterns for other creatures such as mice, rabbits, cats – whatever you fancy. Our animals are sewn together with tiny buttonhole stitches, but if children are making them a simple running stitch is quicker and easier.

Pattern pieces are on pages 96–7.

Owl

Materials

Felt One piece 15 × 13cm [6 × 5in] yellow or orange for body; one piece 6 × 5cm [2½ × 2in] light brown or green for wings and ear tufts; scraps of white, green or brown, black, orange or yellow for eyes and beak
Other items Orange or yellow pipe cleaner for feet; synthetic stuffing; clear glue

Cut pattern pieces in felt as indicated. Place the ear tufts between the body pieces and secure with invisible stitches. Sew across the tail along a–b on right side, then sew body along dotted lines. Stuff well and sew opening closed.
   Stitch a wing to each side seam. Cut 1.5cm [⅝in] diam. white felt circles for eyes and glue or sew in place. Fix a smaller green or brown circle on top and then a black vertical bar for the pupil. Attach the beak.
   Push the pipe cleaner through the body, roughly at a–b. Cut off unwanted length, form ends into loops and sew in position.

Parrot

Materials

Felt One piece 10 × 11cm [4 × 4⅜in] royal blue for body; one piece 14 × 5cm [5½ × 2in] yellow for tail and crest; scraps of red and green for wings; light blue for tail; orange for tail and beak; white for eyes
Other items Two small black beads for pupils; one orange pipe cleaner; synthetic stuffing; clear glue

Cut pattern pieces in felt as indicated. Place crest and beak between body pieces and secure with invisible stitches. Sew body along dotted lines and stuff firmly. Stitch tail pieces together: yellow in center, blue, then orange; insert into body and sew opening closed.
   Sew green wings on top of red ones and stitch in place. Cut two 6mm [¼in] diam. eyes in white felt; glue in place and sew bead on top of each. Push pipe cleaner through body at a, cut off unwanted length and bend under for feet.

What-is-it Bird

Materials

Felt One piece 12 × 8cm [4¾ × 3¼in] red for body; scrap of blue for wings
Other items Two small white feathers for tail; two small black beads for eyes; one yellow pipe cleaner for feet; synthetic stuffing.

Cut the end off one feather to be used for the beak.
   Cut pattern pieces in felt as indicated Secure the beak firmly between the body pieces with a few invisible stitches. Sew along dotted lines and stuff bird at a; insert feathers and sew opening closed.
   Push the pipe cleaner through the bird at b, cut off unwanted length and twist ends into loops to form feet.

Snake

Materials

Felt One piece 28 × 4cm [11 × 1½in] green or light purple for upper body; one piece yellow or pink same size for under body; scraps of red for tongue
Other items Two green or purple sequins for eyes; synthetic stuffing; two pipe cleaners

Cut pattern pieces in felt as indicated. Tack tongue between body pieces. Twist the pipe cleaners together to measure 28cm [11in] and place between body pieces. Start sewing along dotted lines from a around to b and then to c. At c, stuff head firmly. Continue sewing and stuffing as you go along. Make sure pipe cleaners are embedded in the stuffing and cannot be felt from outside. Sew opening closed.
   Sew on two sequins for eyes. Twist snake into shape.

Breakfast Set

Egg cozies and napkin rings in woven felt are child's play to make – especially the napkin rings, which need no sewing.

Egg Cozy

Materials
Felt Two pieces 30 × 14cm [12 × 5½in], one in dark color, one in light color
Cotton 25 × 14cm [10 × 5½in] for lining

Cut a paper pattern to the shape Q.
   Cut the piece of dark felt as in **R** – the cutting lines are 1cm [⅜in] apart, with an uncut border the same size all around. Cut the light felt into strips 14 × 1cm [5½ × ⅜in]. Weave these strips into the dark felt. Fold completed felt piece in half, lay the paper pattern on it, outline and then sew around curved edge. Cut off any surplus felt and turn right side out.
   Use pattern to cut two pieces of cotton for lining. Sew together along curved edge; turn right side out. Slip into cozy. Turn under raw edge and slip stitch to bottom.

Napkin Ring

Materials
Felt Two pieces 13 × 5cm [5 × 2in], one in dark color, one in light color
Clear glue

Weave the napkin ring in the same way as the cozy, turning the loose ends of the woven strips under and gluing them neatly to the back. Overlap short sides 1cm [⅜in] and glue together to complete ring.

Key
All pattern pieces are actual size.
Owl A – body (cut 2); B – wing (cut 2); C – tuft (cut 2); D – beak (cut 1).
Parrot E – body (cut 2); F – crest (cut 1); G – wing (cut 2); H – wing (cut 2); I – beak (cut 1); J – tail (cut 1); K – tail (cut 2); L – tail (cut 2).
What-is-it bird M – body (cut 2); N – wing (cut 2).
Snake O – body (cut 2); P – tongue (cut 1).

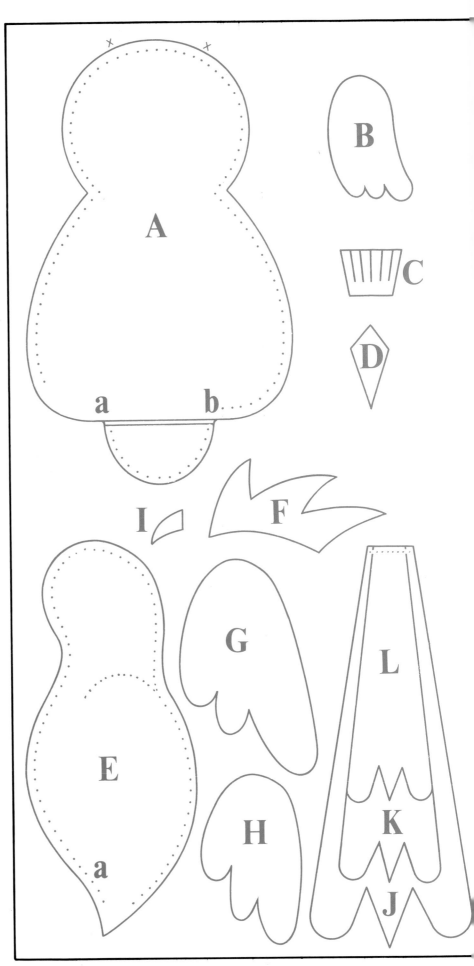

. . . . . sewing line

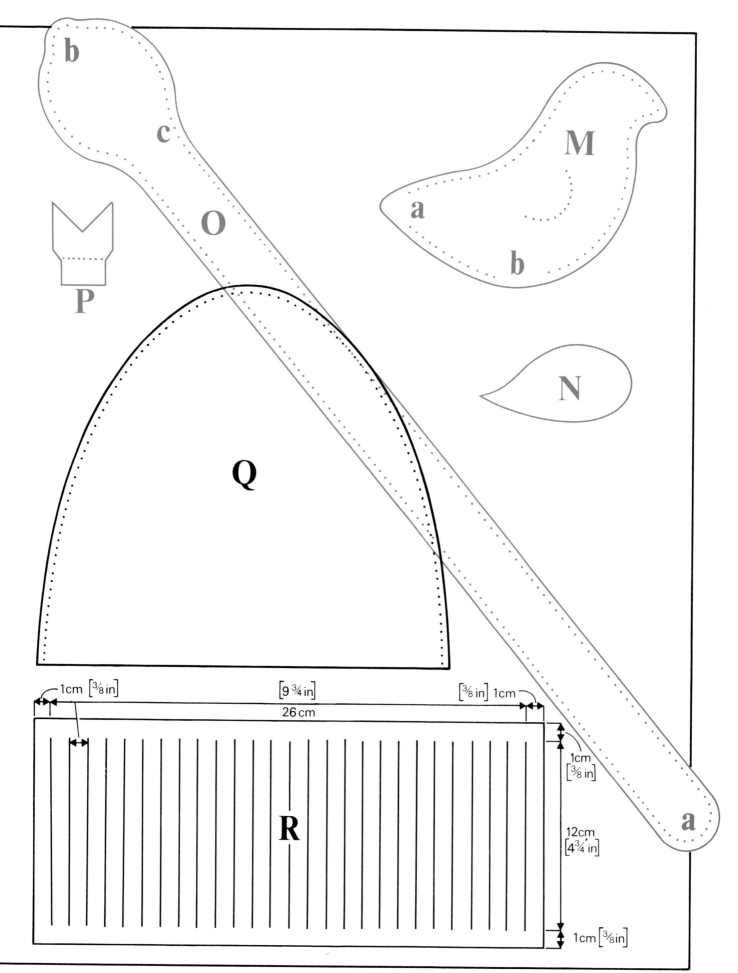

b

c

O

M

a

b

P

N

Q

1cm [³⁄₈ in]   [9 ¾ in]   [³⁄₈ in] 1cm

26 cm

1cm
[³⁄₈ in]

R

12cm
[4¾ in]

a

1cm [³⁄₈ in]

Key Ring Tags

These are great fun to make, as there is no end to the things you can use, and the type of tag you can produce: personalized ones; joke ones; ones that symbolize the recipient's hobby or job. Our picture shows just a few of the possibilities; once started you're bound to think of lots more.

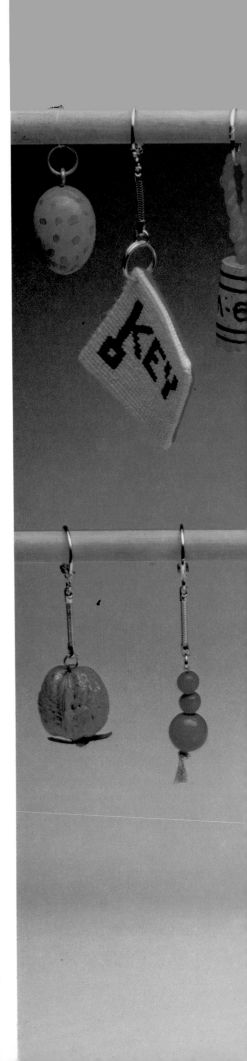

Materials

Rings Metal key rings complete with short chain and jump ring; large and small split rings; small screw eyes
Tags Plywood, canvas, cardboard, wooden egg, ball and beads; walnut; wine bottle cork; tassel; leather
Other items Felt; tapestry yarns; thick and thin cord; leather stripping (thongs); enamel paints; wood stain; varnish; self-adhesive letters; wood-filler; clear glue; strong thread

The materials listed are the ones we used, but anything is suitable that will stand up to wear and tear and can be pierced to attach the key ring. The tags should be easily identifiable by touch, and easy to hold; not angular or rough or they could damage fingers or pocket linings. Size is a matter of taste; some people like them large and easy to find, others prefer something smaller. Our largest are the blue and yellow tapestry squares, 5cm [2in] across.

The main tools needed, apart from

sewing things and a craft knife, are a spike to make holes in the softer materials, and a hand drill for drilling harder ones such as wood. Beads with only a small hole can be filled with wood-filler to take a screw eye. For sawing shapes in plywood, use a fretsaw or coping saw.

To thread cord or leather strips through beads you need a strong large-eyed needle such as a darning or yarn needle. The cord can be secured by knotting and gluing inside; by knotting outside and fraying out the ends; or by cutting off flush and hammering in a small wooden wedge (color this with a felt-tip pen to match the cord).

To sew leather punch holes first with spike, needle or compass point, then use a running stitch and strong thread; sew around twice.

For felt tags, cut pieces slightly larger than the cardboard or plywood shape; glue on, and buttonhole stitch around the edge.

Potted Plants

Buying a potted plant can be quite expensive, but if you already have some in the house you can take cuttings from them to make little presents virtually for nothing; even quite large presents if there is time to let them grow for a few months. Relatively quick-growing plants which should root easily include Tradescantia, Impatiens, Coleus, vines such as Grape Ivy and Kangaroo Vine, Crassula, small-leaved

1

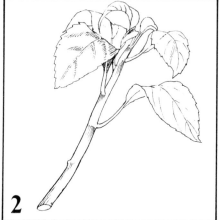

2

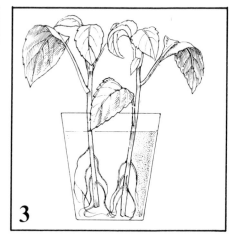

3

4

5

6

philodendrons, ivies and pelargoniums. All these plants need trimming anyway to keep them bushy, so in trying to root the cuttings you have nothing to lose. The best time for taking cuttings is spring or late summer.

1   This large plant (Impatiens) is getting straggly and could do with having some of its long new growths shortened to encourage new shoots from the base.
2   To get the trimmings to grow into new plants, cut them about 10cm [4in] long with a sharp knife, just below a leaf bud. Trim away leaves from lower third of the cutting.
3   Place in a glass or bottle of water and leave for several weeks. The advantage of this method is that you can see if and when roots start to form.
4   When the cuttings have developed a

bushy root growth, plant in potting soil in the smallest-sized plastic pots. Leave for a week or two to settle down.
5   If you want to give a larger plant, leave for a couple of months to grow. The plant is ready for the next-size pot when roots peep out of the drain holes.
6   After repotting leave for a week or two to settle down. Present the plant complete with a label giving its name and the conditions it likes – just like the ones in the florist's shop.

Knitting

Abbreviations

alt	alternate	sl	slip
beg	beginning	st(s)	stitch(es)
dec	decrease	st st	stocking (stockinette) st
inc	increase	tbl	through back of loop
K	knit	tog	together
P	purl	bind off	cast off
pat	pattern		
psso	pass slip st over		
rep	repeat		

pat pattern *Note* Both metric and American sizes of needle are given in the following patterns.

Cuddly Panda and Koala

Both these delightful toys are knitted from the same pattern. The complete change of character is achieved by changing the yarn color, molding the head shape differently when stuffing, and giving the koala bear his distinctive nose and claws, and the panda his eye patches.

Panda

Materials
Knitting worsted (brushed Aran) yarn:
50g [2oz] in black
50g [2oz] in white
3¾mm [No. 4] knitting needles
One pair lock-in safety eyes
Stuffing

Size
Height 29cm [11½in]

Gauge
5½ sts × 9 rows = 2.5cm [1in] in garter st

Head (make two)
With white yarn cast on 14 sts. K 1 row.
1st, 5th and 9th rows Inc 1, K to last st, inc 1.
2nd and alt rows Knit.
3rd and 7th rows Inc 1, K to end.
10th to 12th rows Knit.
13th row As 1st. Rep last 4 rows once more, then K 3 rows = 26 sts.
Inc 1 st at beg of next and following 4th row = 28 sts.
K 3 rows.
Shape nose Bind off 7 sts, K to last 2 sts,

K2 tog. K 1 row.
Next row K2 tog, K to last 2 sts, K2 tog, K 1 row.
Rep last 2 rows until 8 sts remain. Bind off.

Gusset (make one)

With white yarn (starting at back neck) cast on 10 sts. K 5 rows.
Next row Inc 1, K to last st, inc 1.
Rep last 6 rows twice more = 16 sts.
K 17 rows.
Next row K2 tog, K to last 2 sts, K2 tog, K 7 rows.
Rep last 8 rows three times more, then dec row once more = 6 sts.
K 11 rows.
Next row K2 tog, K2, K2 tog.
Next row K2 tog twice. Bind off.

Ears (make two)

With black yarn cast on 11 sts; K 3 rows.
Next row Inc 1, K to last st, inc 1, K6 rows.
Next row K2 tog, K to last 2 sts, K2 tog, K 1 row.
Rep last 2 rows until 7 sts remain. Bind off.

Eyes (make two)

With black yarn cast on 6 sts. K 1 row.
1st, 5th and 9th rows K2 tog, K to last st, inc 1.
2nd and alt rows Knit.
3rd and 7th rows K to last st, inc 1.
11th, 13th and 15th rows K2 tog, K to last 2 sts, K2 tog. Bind off.

Body Front (make one)

With white yarn cast on 17 sts. K 1 row.
Next row Inc 1, K to last st, inc 1, K 3 rows.
Rep last 4 rows 4 times more = 27 sts.
K 20 rows. Break off white, join black.
K 1 row. Cast on 7 sts at beg of next 2 rows.
Next row Inc 1, K to last st, inc 1.
K 1 row. Rep last 2 rows once more = 45 sts.
K 13 rows. Bind off 4 sts at beg of next 2 rows. Bind off 3 sts at beg of next 4 rows = 25 sts.
K2 tog at each end of next 2 rows. Break black. With white yarn, rep last 2 rows once more = 17 sts. K 2 rows. Bind off.

Legs (make four)

With black cast on 16 sts. K 1 row.
1st row K2 tog, K to last st, inc 1.
K 3 rows. Rep last 4 rows once more.
9th row K2 tog, K to end. K 3 rows.
Rep last 4 rows once more = 14 sts.

17th row K2 tog, K to last 2 sts, K2 tog.
Bind off 4 sts at beg of row at same edge twice.
Bind off remaining sts.

Right Back (make one)

With white yarn cast on 14 sts. K 1 row.
1st row Inc 1, K to last st, inc 1. K 3 rows. Rep last 4 rows twice more.
13th row Inc 1, K to end. K 3 rows. Rep last 4 rows once = 22 sts. K 20 rows.
Break off white, join black, K 2 rows.
Cast on 7 sts at beg of next row. K 1 row.
Next row Inc 1, K to last 2 sts, K2 tog.
K 1 row. Rep last 2 rows once = 29 sts.
Next row K to last 2 sts, K2 tog, K3 rows. Rep last 4 rows twice, then 1st 2 rows once more = 25 sts.
Next row Bind off 4 sts, K to last 2 sts, K2 tog. K 1 row.
Next row Bind off 3 sts, K to last 2 sts, K2 tog. K 1 row. Rep last 2 rows once more = 12 sts.
Next row K2 tog, K to end. K 1 row.
Break off black. With white, rep last 2 rows once. K 2 rows. Bind off.

Left Back (make one)

Work as for right back, reversing shapings.

Finishing

Sew leg slope to lower body slope on front and backs. Sew backs to front.
Sew center back seam, leaving opening at lower edge for stuffing. Sew eye to side head, with cast-on edge to gusset edge above nose. Starting at nose, sew head gusset to side heads. Sew seam from nose to neck. Insert eyes and stuff head. Sew on ears. Stuff limbs and sew head to body. Stuff body and close back seam. Embroider nose and mouth.

Koala Bear

Materials

100g [4oz] knitting worsted (brushed Aran) yarn
Scrap of mohair to match, for ears
3¾mm [No. 4] knitting needles
One pair lock-in safety eyes
One plastic nose
Scraps of black felt for claws (or buy plastic ones)
Stuffing

Make as for panda but using one color throughout and omitting eye pieces.
Use mohair yarn for the ears to give a fluffy look. When finishing, insert plastic nose at same time as eyes.
Place eyes close in to nose as in the picture.

Fair Isle Pullover

Combining traditional-style patterns with decidedly untraditional colors, this Fair Isle pullover looks equally good on a man or woman. It can be made in four different sizes.

Materials

4-ply fingering yarn:
150(150:175:175)g [6(6:7:7)oz] in main color
50g [2oz] all sizes, in gold, dark brown, fawn
25g [1oz] all sizes, in cream, green, red, med. brown
2¾mm and 3¼mm [No. 2 and No. 3] knitting needles

Sizes

Actual size 94(99:104:109)cm
[37(39:41:43)in]
Length 56(58.5:61:63.5)cm
22(23:24:25)in]

Gauge

7 sts × 9 rows = 2.5cm [1in] with 3¼mm [No. 3] needles and st st

Back

With main color and 2¾mm [No. 2] needles cast on 126(132:138:144) sts and work 27 rows in K1, P1 rib.
Inc row Rib 13(16:19:22) * inc 1 in next st, rib 19; rep 4 times more, inc 1 in next st, rib 12(15:18:21) = 132(138:144:150) sts.
Change to 3¼mm [No. 3] needles and work Fair Isle pattern from chart, starting required size and repeating pat until work measures 32(33:34.5:35.5)cm [12½(13:13½:14)in]. **
Maintaining pat bind off 11(12:13:14) sts at beg of next 2 rows. Dec 1 st at each end of every row until 92(96:100:104) sts remain. Work without further shaping until armhole measures 24(25.5:26.5:28)cm [9½(10:10½:11)in]. Bind off 8(8:9:9) sts at beg of next 4 rows; bind off 8(9:8:9) sts at beg of next 2 rows. Place 44(46:48:50) sts on spare needle.

Front

Work as for back to **. Bind off
11(12:13:14) sts at beg of next 2 rows.
Divide for neck K2 tog, pat 51(53:55:
57), K2 tog, turn. Place remaining sts
on spare needle. Cont in pat, dec 1 st at
armhole edge on every row 8 (8 : 8 : 8)
times more, and at the same time dec
1 st at neck edge on every 4th row until
31(32:33:34) sts remain. Then dec 1 st
at neck edge every 3rd row until
24(25 : 26 : 27) sts remain. Work
without further shaping until armhole
is the same depth as back armhole,
ending at armhole edge. Bind off
8(8 : 9 : 9) sts at beg of next and
following alt rows. Bind off remaining
sts. Return to other sts and complete as
for first side, reversing all shapings.

Neck Edging

Join left shoulder seam. With 2¾mm
[No. 2] needles and main color K44
(46:48:50) sts from back neck; pick
up 65(67:69:71) sts down left side of
neck; 1 st from center point (mark this st
with colored thread), and 65(67:69:71)
sts up right side of neck = 175(181:187:
193) sts. Work 1 row in rib. Work 10
rows in rib, dec 1 st each side of marked
st on every row. Bind off in rib.

Armhole Edging

Join right shoulder seam. With 2¾mm
[No. 2] needles and main color pick up
146(150:154:158) sts along armhole
edge and work 12 rows in K1, P1 rib.
Bind off in rib.

Finishing

Join side seams.

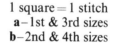

1 square = 1 stitch
a – 1st & 3rd sizes
b – 2nd & 4th sizes

■ gold   ■ green

■ dark brown   ■ red

▨ fawn   ▨ medium brown

□ cream   □ main color

105

Hooded Car Coat

This stunning knitted car coat takes a lot of yarn and quite a bit of knitting, but the end result is something for an experienced knitter to be proud of. The tweedy, bulky yarn and bold diagonal pattern give it a sporty, go-anywhere look.

Materials

1050(1100 : 1150)g [38(40 : 42)oz] bulky yarn
Seven buttons
5½mm and 6mm [No. 8 and No. 9] knitting needles
Optional – for fringe 50g [2oz] mohair 4mm [No. 5] knitting needles

Sizes

Actual size 96(101 : 106)cm [38(40 : 42)in]
Length 71(73.5 : 73.5)cm [28(29 : 29)in]
Sleeve with cuff turned back 46cm [18in]

Gauge

15 sts × 18 rows = 10cm [4in] with 6mm [No. 9] needles and pat

Abbreviations

Inc 1 K into front and back of st
Cross 2 K into 2nd st on needle then into 1st st
Tw 2r (twist 2 right) K into 2nd st, then P into 1st st
Tw 2l (twist 2 left) P into 2nd st on needle, behind 1st st, then K into 1st st
Note Knitted sts must remain on front of work.

Back

With 5½mm [No. 8] needles cast on 66(70 : 74) sts and work 11 rows in garter st.
Inc row K3(5 : 7) * inc 1, K11; rep from * 5 times, inc 1, K2(4 : 6) = 72(76 : 80) sts. Change to 6mm [No. 9] needles and pat starting with wrong side facing.
1st row K0(2 : 4) * K2, P2, K2, rep from * to last O(2 : 4) sts, knit.
2nd row P0(2 : 4) * P2, cross 2, P2, rep from * to last O(2 : 4) sts, purl.
3rd and alt. rows K the K sts, P the P sts.
4th row P0(2 : 4) * Pl, tw 2r, tw 2l, Pl, rep from * to last O(2 : 4) sts, purl.
6th row P0(2 : 4) * tw 2r, P2, tw 2l; rep from * to last O(2 : 4) sts, purl.
8th row P0(2 : 4), K1 * P4, cross 2, rep from * to last 5(7 : 9) sts, P4, K1, PO

(2 : 4).
10th row P0(2 : 4) * tw 2l, P2, tw 2r; rep from * to last O(2 : 4) sts, purl.
12th row P0(2 : 4) * Pl, tw 2l, tw 2r, P1; rep from * to last O(2 : 4) sts, purl.
These 12 rows form pat and are repeated throughout garment. Work without further shaping until back measures 43(46 : 46)cm [17(18 : 18)in]. Adjust length here.
Bind off 5 sts at beg of next 2 rows = 62(66 : 70) sts. Work without further shaping until armhole measures 24cm [9½in].
Divide sts for neck Pat 20(21 : 22). Bind off 22(24 : 26) sts, pat 20(21 : 22), place sts on spare needle.

Pocket Lining (make two)

With 6mm [No. 9] needles cast on 18 sts and starting with a K row work 20 rows in st st. Place sts on spare needle.

Left Front

With 5½mm [No. 8] needles cast on 41(43 : 45) sts and work 11 rows in garter st.
Inc row K3(5 : 7) * inc 1, K11, twice, inc 1, K to end = 44(46,48) sts. Change to 6mm [No. 9] needles and pat as for back:
1st row K8, * K2, P2, K2; rep from * to last O(2 : 4) sts, knit.
Keeping 8 sts at front edge in garter st for border, work in pat for 19 more rows, ending at front edge.

Pocket

K8, pat 12, slip next 18 sts on to a safety pin and set aside, K18 sts from lining pat 6(8 : 10). Work without further shaping in pat until front matches back to armhole, ending at side edge. Bind off 5 sts at beg of next row, work straight until armhole measures 16.5cm [6½in], ending at front edge.

Neck

Bind off 11(12 : 13) sts, pat to end. Dec 1 st at neck edge on every row 4 times, and on every alt row 4 times = 20(21 : 22) sts. When armhole matches back, bind off shoulder sts, together with back shoulder sts loosely.

Right Front

Work as for left front reversing all shapings and making seven buttonholes in border on 4th row and evenly spaced to neck (about every 20th row).
Buttonhole row Right side facing, K3, bind off 2, K3 = 8 sts, pat to end.
Next row Pat to last 8 sts, K3, cast on 2, K3.

Pocket Edging

With 5½mm [No. 8] needles slip sts for pocket top on to needle. Work 9 rows in garter st, bind off.

Sleeves

With 5½mm [No. 8] needles cast on 48 sts (for all sizes) and work 18 rows in garter st.
Inc row K6 * inc 1, K11; rep from * 3 times, inc 1, K5 = 52 sts. Change to 6mm [No. 9] needles and pat.
1st row K2 * K2, P2, K2; rep from * to last 2 sts, K2.
Work in pat, increasing 1st each end of 5th and every following 6th row until 76 sts are on needle, working extra sts into pat. Work until sleeve measures 46cm [18in] from start of pat.

Dec row K2 * K2 tog, K12; rep from * to last 4 sts, K2 tog, K2. Work 8 rows in garter st. Bind off loosely.

Hood
With 5½mm [No. 8] needles cast on 96 sts and work 5 rows in garter st.
Inc row K3 * inc 1, K9; rep from * to last 3 sts, inc 1, K2 = 106 sts. Change to 6mm [No. 9] needles and pat.
1st row K2 * K2, P2, K2; rep from * to last 2 sts, K2.
Working in pat, dec 1 st each end of next and following 4th row = 102 sts. Work without further shaping until 2 complete pats are worked.
Shape head Right side facing pat 49, P2 tog, P2 tog, pat 49.
2nd row Pat 48, K2 tog, K2 tog, pat 48.
Dec 2 sts in this way 5 times more = 88 sts. Then dec 2 sts on every alt row only until 70 sts remain.
Next row Pat 35 sts, turn. Place sts tog and bind off tog on wrong side of work.

Finishing
Pin center of sleeve top to shoulder seam. Sew sleeves into armhole, sewing edge of garter st to bound off sts. Join sleeve and side seams. Hem pocket lining. Hem pocket edging at sides. Pin edge of hood to center front border, and center back to center back neck. Ease fullness evenly around neck and sew together. Sew on buttons.

Zippered Jacket

This knitted leisure jacket makes a perfect present for a teenager, boy or girl, to wear with jeans or sportswear. The cable pattern is based on a traditional design used on Irish fishermen's sweaters for generations.

Materials

650(650 : 700)g [24(24 : 26)oz] lightweight 4-ply Aran yarn
46(48 : 51)cm [18(19 : 20)in] open-end zipper
4½mm and 3¾mm [No. 6 and No. 4] knitting needles; double-pointed cable needle

Sizes

To fit 86(91 : 96)cm [34(36 : 38)in] bust/chest
Length 51(53.5 : 57)cm [20(21 : 22½)in]
Sleeve 46(46 : 48)cm [18(18 : 19)in]

Gauge

20 sts × 24 rows = 10cm [4in] in Irish moss stitch with 4½mm [No. 6] needles

Stitches

Irish Moss (Aran Rice) Stitch
1st and 2nd rows * K1, P1, rep from * to end.
3rd and 4th rows * P1, K1, rep from * to end.
Cable Pattern
1st, 3rd, 5th and 9th rows P3, K12, P3.
2nd, 4th, 6th, 8th and 10th rows K3, P12, K3.
7th row P3, cable 6B (sl 3 sts on to cable needle to back of work, K3, K sts from cable needle), cable 6F (sl 3 sts on to cable needle to front of work, K3, K sts from cable needle), P3.

Back

With 3¾mm [No. 4] needles cast on 88(94 : 100) sts and work 18 rows in

K1, P1 rib. Change to 4½mm [No. 6] needles and Irish moss st; work until back measures 32(33 : 37)cm [12½ (13 : 14½)in]. Bind off 4 sts at beg of next 2 rows.
Shape raglan: 1st row K3, K2 tog tbl, pat to last 5 sts, K2 tog, K3.
2nd row K3, P1, pat to last 4 sts, P1, K3.
Rep last 2 rows until 24(28 : 32) sts remain. Bind off.

Sleeves

With 3¾mm [No. 4] needles cast on 46(48 : 50) sts and work 18 rows in K1, P1 rib. Change to 4½mm [No. 6] needles and start pat as follows:
1st row Moss 14(15 : 16) sts. Work 18 sts in cable pat, moss 14(15 : 16).
Maintaining pat, inc 1 st each end of 7th and every following 6th row until 72(76 : 78) sts are on needle. Work without further shaping until sleeve measures 46(46 : 48)cm [18(18 : 19)in]. Bind off 4 sts at beg of next 2 rows. Shape raglan as for back until 8(10 : 10) sts remain. Bind off.

Left Front

With 3¾mm [No. 4] needles cast on
46(50:54) sts and work 18 rows in K1,
P1 rib, keeping 3 sts at front edge in
garter st. Change to 4½mm [No. 6]
needles and pat.

1st row Moss 25(29:33), work 18 sts in
cable pat, K3.

Still keeping 3 sts in garter st at front
edge, work 10 rows in pat ending at
front edge.

Divide for pocket Pat 40(42:44), turn,
place remaining 6(8:10) sts on holder.
Dec 1 st at pocket edge on next and alt
rows until 28(30:32) sts remain,
ending at pocket edge.

Pocket lining With 4½mm [No. 6]
needles cast on 22 sts (for all sizes)
and work 10 rows in st st starting with
a K row. Now pat 6(8:10) sts from
holder on to same needle.

Work on these 28(30:32) sts taking 1st
into moss pat on next and alt rows,
working remaining sts in st st. Work 23
rows, ending at pocket edge. Bind off
10 sts, pat to end.

Work across all sts until front matches
back to armhole, ending at side edge.
Bind off 4 sts, pat to end. Work 1 row.

1st row K3, K2 tog tbl, pat to end.

2nd row Pat to last 4 sts, P1, K3.

Rep last 2 rows until 22(24:28) sts
remain, ending at front edge.

Bind off 7(9:11) sts, pat to end. Dec
1 st at neck edge on next 3(3:5) rows and
on following 4(4:4) alt rows, keeping
raglan shaping correct until all sts
are worked.

Right Front

Work as for left front, reversing all
shapings and pat.

Pocket Edgings

With 3¼mm [No. 3] needles, cast on
28 sts and work 8 rows in K1, P1 rib.
Bind off.

Collar

With 3¾mm [No. 4] needles, cast on
95(99:105) sts.

1st row K3 * P1, K1; rep from * to last
4 sts, P1, K3.

2nd row K3 * K1, P1; rep from * to last
4 sts, K4.

Rep last 2 rows 12(13:14) times.
Bind off.

Finishing

Join raglan seams. Join side and sleeve
seams. Sew bound-off edge of pocket
edgings to pocket slope; hem lining in
place. Sew bound-off edge of collar
to neck. Sew in zipper.

Toddler's Tank Top and Patchwork Sweater

The motif on this simple little tank top is embroidered – much easier than working a knitted pattern.

Materials

75g [3oz] 4-ply fingering yarn
Scraps of tapestry of 4-ply yarn for embroidery
3mm and 2¼mm [No. 2 and No. 0] knitting needles

Sizes

To fit 51(56)cm [20(22in)] chest
Length 28(30)cm [11(12)in]

Gauge

30 sts × 38 rows = 10 × 10cm [4 × 4in] st st with 3mm [No. 2] needles

Back

With 2¼mm [No. 0] needles cast on 80(86) sts and work single rib for 14 rows. Change to 3mm [No. 2] needles and st st; starting with a K row work until back measures 16.5(19)cm [6½(7½)in] ending with P row. *Shape armhole* Bind off 6(7) sts at beg of next 2 rows. Dec 1 st each end of every row 3 times, and every alt row until 52(56) sts remain. Continue without further shaping until back measures 26.5(29)cm [10½(11½)in]. Bind off 6(6) sts at beg of next 2 rows, then 5(6) sts at beg of next 2 rows. Place remaining 30(32) sts on spare needle for back neck.

Front

Work as for back until armhole shaping is completed = 52(56) sts.
Shape neck K15(16), K2 tog. Leave remaining sts on holder. Dec 1 st at neck edge on next 2 rows, then dec 1 st at same edge on alt rows until 11(12) sts remain. Work without further shaping until front matches back to shoulder shaping, ending at armhole edge. Bind off 6(6) sts, work to end. Work 1 row. Bind off remaining sts. Return to other side and slip 18(20) sts on to thread for center neck. Starting neck edge K2 tog, K to end. Complete as for first half of neck, reversing shapings.

110

Embroidery

Each square on chart for motif (diagram 2) represents a stitch on knitting, and each symbol represents a color. Mark position of motif with tacking sts. Starting at the lowest point on chart, embroider motif on knitting as shown in diagram 1.

Neck Edging

Join left shoulder seam on wrong side of work. With 2¼mm [No. 0] needles and right side of work facing K30(32) sts from back neck, pick up and K29 (30) sts down side of neck; K across 18(20) sts at center front neck and pick up and K29(30) sts up other side of neck = 106(112) sts. Work 10 rows in single rib. Bind off loosely in rib.

Armholes

Join other shoulder seam. With 2¼mm [No. 0] needles pick up and K86(88) sts around armhole edge. Work 10 rows in single rib. Bind off in rib.

Finishing

Join neckband seam. Join side seams.

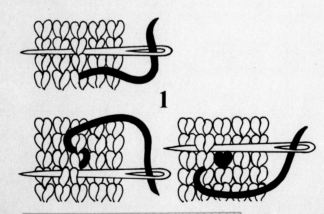

1

2

111

1

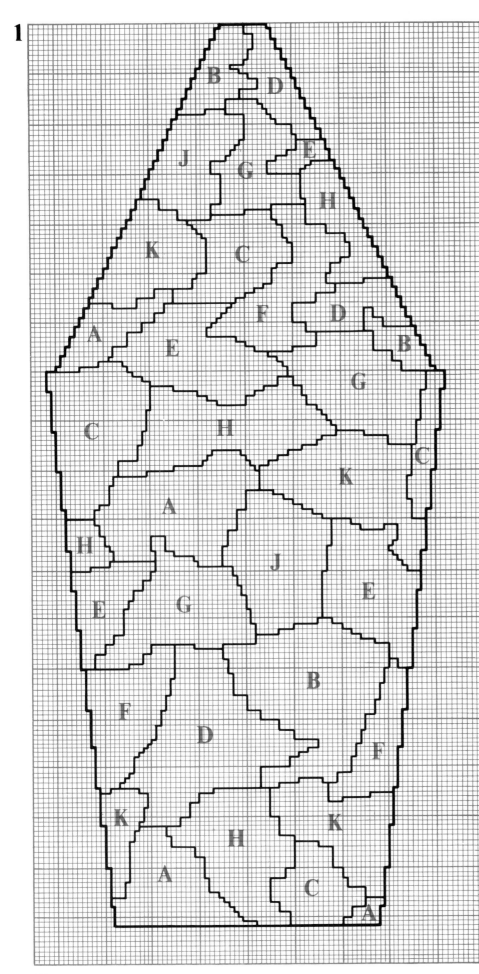

Patchwork Sweater

The 'patches' on this beautiful sweater have been carefully worked out to carry over the seams, giving a highly professional look.

Materials

Knitting worsted (double knitting) yarn:
125g [5oz] in main color K
50g [2oz] in colors A, B, C, D, E, F, G, H
25g [1oz] in color J
3mm and 3¾mm [No. 2 and No. 4] knitting needles

Size

To fit 96cm [38in] bust
Length 56cm [22in]
Sleeve length 44.5cm [17½in]

Gauge

23 sts × 32 rows = 10cm [4in] st st with 3¾mm [No. 4] needles

Back

With 3mm [No. 2] needles and main color cast on 108 sts; work 20 rows in K2, P2 rib. Change to 3¾mm [No. 4] needles and st st. Work pat from chart, twisting yarn tog before starting next color to avoid holes. Shape raglan on alt rows as chart. Place sts on spare needle for neck.

Front

Work as for back, following raglan and V-neck shaping as directed on chart.

Sleeves

With 3mm [No. 2] needles and main color cast on 56 sts; work 24 rows in K2, P2 rib. Change to 3¾mm [No. 4] needles and st st. Work pat and increases as directed on chart. Shape raglan. Place remaining sts on spare needle.

Neck

With right side facing and 3mm [No. 2] needles, main color, K across sts for back neck and one sleeve; pick up 52 sts down left side of neck, 2 sts from center V (mark these 2 with coloured thread), 52 sts up right side of neck, and K across other sleeve = 160 sts. Work in K2, P2 rib (marked sts should be purled on 1st row), dec 1 st each side of marked sts on every row. Work 11 rows in all. Bind off in rib.

2

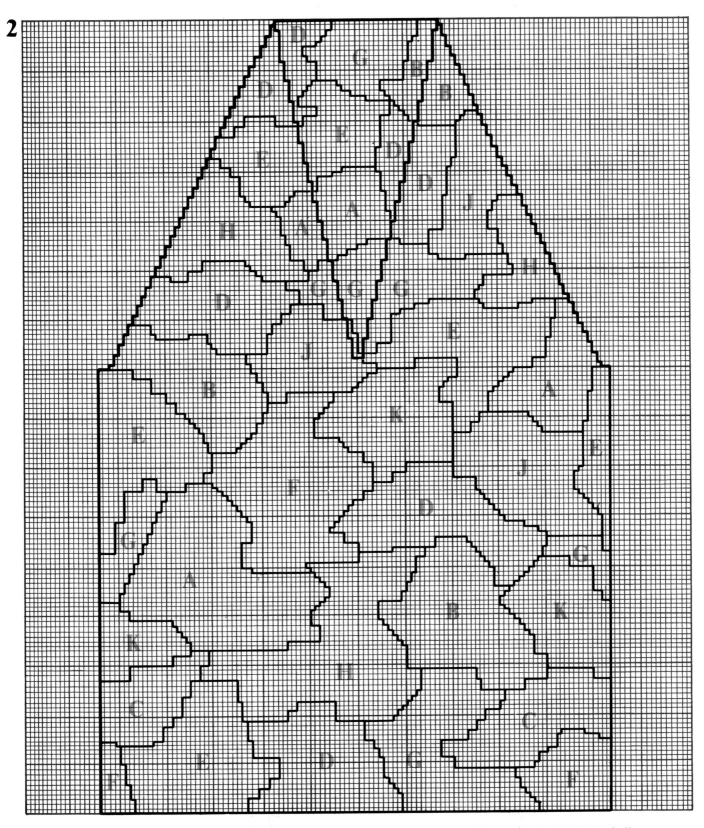

1 square = 1 stitch in both diagrams
diagram 1 – sleeve
diagram 2 – front and back

Finishing
Weave loose ends in neatly to avoid
holes. Joining all seams with
appropriate color, sew raglans. Join
side and sleeve seams.

113

Winter Warmers

Hat, scarf and mittens knitted in sock-it-to-me colors keep the wearer cheerful as well as warm!

Materials
Lightweight 4-ply Aran yarn:
400g [14oz] in main color
100g [4oz] in green
50g [2oz] in red and white
5½mm, 5mm and 4mm [No. 8, No. 7 and No. 5] knitting needles

Size
To fit an average woman.

Gauge
3 sts × 6 rows = 2.5cm [1in] using 5½mm [No. 8] needles and pat

Hat
With 5½mm [No. 8] needles and main color cast on 33 sts.
1st row K into front and back of every st (66 sts).
Pat row Sl 1 as if to knit, * K1 below, K1; rep from * to last K1. Rep pat row until work measures 23cm [9in].
Stripes 6 rows green, 4 rows red, 2 rows white, 4 rows red, 6 rows green. Continue in main color until work measures 56cm [22in].
Next row * K2 tog; rep from * to end.
Next row K1 * P2 tog; rep from * to end. Thread yarn through sts and draw up.

Finishing
Sew side seam. Fold hat in half, gather cast on edge and draw up. Fasten off inside crown. Fold stripe pat back for brim.

Scarf
With 5½mm [No. 8] needles and main color cast on 30 sts. K 1 row.
Pat row Sl 1 as if to knit * K1 below. K1; rep to last st, K1. Rep pat row throughout, work 40 rows in main color.
Stripes 18 rows green, 10 rows red, 6 rows white, 10 rows red, 18 rows green.

Continue in main color for 100cm
[39½in]. Rep stripe pat then work 40
rows in main color. Bind off in rib.
Fringe Cut yarn into 38cm [15in]
lengths and knot 4 strands tog through
ends of scarf.

Mittens
Right Hand
With 4mm [No. 5] needles and main
color cast on 32 sts and work 7.5cm
[3in] in K1, P1 rib. Change to 5mm
[No. 7] needles and pat as for hat.
Work 4 rows. **
Inc row Pat 16 (inc 2, by working into
front, back and front of next st) twice.
Pat 14. Work 9 rows in pat.
Next row Pat 16, inc 2, pat 4, inc 2,
pat 14. Work 9 rows in pat.
Shape thumb Pat 25, turn, cast on 2 sts.
Next row Pat 11 sts, turn. Work 5cm
[2in] on these 11 sts.
Shape top Work 2 tog all across row.
Thread yarn through sts, draw up and
join seam.
With right side of work facing pick up
3 sts from base of thumb. Pat 15.
Work across all 34 sts for 7 rows.
Work stripes as for hat. Continue in
main color, work 12 rows.
Shape top * Work 2 tog, rep from * to
end.
Next row * P2 tog, rep from * to last
st, K1.
Thread yarn through sts, draw up and
join side seam.

Left Hand
Work as for right hand to **.
Inc row Pat 14, (inc 2) twice, pat 16.
Work as for right hand reversing all
shapings.

Toddler's Hat and Mittens

(For picture see page 15)

Materials
75g [3oz] lightweight knitting worsted (double knitting) yarn
3¼mm and 4mm [No. 3 and No. 5] knitting needles

Size
To fit 2–3 years

Hat
With 3¼mm [No. 3] needles cast on 100 sts and work 7½cm [3in] in K1, P1 rib. Change to 4mm [No. 5] needles and work in garter st until hat measures 20cm [8in] from beg.
Shape top: 1st row * K2, K2 tog; rep from * to end.
2nd row K1 * K2 tog; rep from * to end.
3rd row * K2 tog; rep from * to end.
4th row as 2nd.
Thread yarn through sts, draw up and join side seam.

Mittens
Right Hand
With 3¼mm [No. 3] needles cast on 26 sts and work 5cm [2in] in K1, P1 rib. Change to 4mm [No. 5] needles and garter st; K2 rows. *
Inc row K12, inc 1, K2, inc 1, K10. K 3 rows.
Inc row K12, inc 1, K4, inc 1, K10. K 3 rows.
Thumb K19, turn, cast on 2 sts and K9. Work 2.5cm [1in] on these 9 sts.
Next row K1 * K2 tog; rep from * to end. Thread yarn through sts, draw up and join thumb seam.
Pick up 3 sts from base of thumb, K remaining 11 sts = 26 sts. Work in garter st until mitten measures 6·5cm [2½in] from base of thumb.
Shape top * K2 tog; rep from * to end.
Next row K1 * K2 tog; rep from * to end. Thread yarn through sts, draw up and join side seam.

Left Hand
Work as for right hand until * is reached.
Next row K10, inc 1, K2, inc 1, K12. Work as for right hand reversing all shapings.

Slipper Socks

Brightly patterned knitted socks stitched on to a leather sole are fun to wear around the house; warm and comfortable too. The ones in the picture are a medium women's size, but the pattern can easily be adjusted to fit a larger or smaller foot.

Materials
Knitting worsted (double knitting) yarn:
75g [3oz] in black
25g [1oz] in blue, red, yellow and green
3mm and 3¾mm [No. 2 and No. 4] knitting needles
One pair slipper-sock soles

Gauge
24 sts × 32 rows = 10cm [4in] with 3¾mm [No. 4] needles and st st.

With black yarn and 3mm [No. 2] needles cast on 72 sts and work 5cm [2in] in K1, Pl rib. Change to 3¾mm [No. 4] needles and pat as chart, starting at row 1 and working K rows from right to left; P rows from left to right on chart. Work without further shaping until sock measures 25cm [10in]. Adjust leg length here.

Bind off 5 sts at beg of next 2 rows. Maintaining pat, dec 1 st at each end of next and following alt rows until 36 sts remain. Continue straight until sock measures 10cm [4im] from end of shaping. Adjust foot length here.

Dec 1 st at each end of every row until 18 sts remain. Bind off 3 sts at beg of next 4 rows. Bind off remaining sts.

Finishing

Join leg seam. Sew sock to slipper sole.

Diagram shows 12 stitch repeat pattern. Colors are as for pattern except for the blank squares which represent the main color.

1 square = 1 stitch

a – row 1

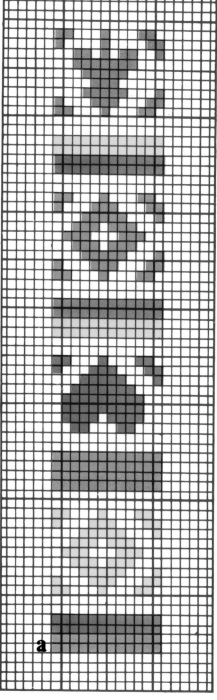

Family Sweaters

With this easy-to-follow pattern in nine sizes you can knit a whole family of sweaters, to suit male or female, young or old, little or large.

Materials
Knitting worsted (double knitting) yarn 200(200 : 250 : 250 : 300 : 350 : 350 : 400 : 450)g [8(8 : 10 : 10 : 12 : 14 : 14 : 16 : 18)oz] in main color
50(50 : 50 : 75 : 75 : 75 : 100 : 100 : 100)g [2(2 : 2 : 3 : 3 : 3 : 4 : 4 : 4)oz] in color A
50(75 : 75 : 100 : 100 : 100 : 125 : 125 : 125)g [2(3 : 3 : 4 : 4 : 4 : 5 : 5 : 5)oz] in color B
3¼mm and 4mm [No. 3 and No. 5] knitting needles

Sizes
Actual sizes
71(76 : 81 : 86 : 91 : 96 : 101 : 106 : 111)cm [28(30 : 32 : 34 : 36 : 38 : 40 : 42 : 44)in]
Length
42 (46 : 49.5 : 53 : 57 : 59.5 : 62 : 65 : 66)cm [16½(18 : 19½ : 21 : 22½ : 23½ : 24½ : 25½ : 26)in]
Sleeve
35.5(38 : 40.5 : 43 : 44.5 : 46 : 48 : 48 : 48)cm [14(15 : 16 : 17 : 17½ : 18 : 19 : 19 : 19)in]

Gauge
23 sts × 28 rows = 10cm [4in] in st st with 4mm [No. 5] needles

Stitches
Garter st : every row knit. Double moss st : K2, P2 for 2 rows : P2, K2 for 2 rows.

Back and Front (alike)
With 4mm [No. 5] needles and main color cast on 82(90 : 98 : 106 : 114 : 120 : 126 : 132 : 134) sts and starting with a K row work 6(6 : 8 : 8 : 10 : 10 : 12 : 12 : 14) rows in st st. * With color A work 6 rows in garter st (all sizes). With color B, K 1 row. Work 10(12 : 12 : 14 : 14 : 16 : 16 : 18 : 18) rows in double moss st. With color A, P 6 rows. With main color and starting with a P row, work 19(19 : 21 : 21 : 23 : 23 : 25 : 25 : 27) rows in st st. * Rep from * to * twice, ending last repeat with 7(7 : 7 : 9 : 9 : 9 : 11 : 11 : 11) rows in main color. Bind off loosely.

Welt
With 3¼mm [No. 3] needles and main color pick up 78(84 : 88 : 94 : 100 : 106 : 112 : 118 : 124) sts along one edge of row ends and work 13(13 : 13 : 13 : 15 : 15 : 15 : 15 : 15) rows in K1, P1 rib. Bind off in rib.

Neck

With 3¼mm [No. 3] needles and main color pick up 78(84:88:94:100:106: 112:118:124) sts along opposite row ends and work 10(10:10:12:12:12: 14:14:14) rows in garter st. K16(17: 19:21:23:25:27:29:31); bind off 46(50:50:52:54:56:58:60:62) sts. K to end. Bind off both sets of shoulder sts tog on wrong side of work.

Sleeves

With 3¼mm [No. 3] needles and main color cast on 40(42:44:48:52:54:56: 58:62) sts and work 14(14:14:16:16: 18:18:18:18) rows in K1, P1 rib. Change to 4mm [No. 5] needles and st st. Inc 1 st each end of 5th and every following 6th row until 56(56:56:60: 64:66:68:68:72) sts are on needle. Then inc 1 st each end of every following 4th row until 66(72:78:84:90:96: 102:106:110) are on needle. Work straight until sleeve measures 32(34: 37:39.5:40.5:42:44.5:44.5:44.5) [12½(13½:14½:15½:16:16½:17½: 17½:17½)in].
Work 10 rows more, inc 1 st at *beg* of every row = 76(82:88:94:100: 106:112:116:120) sts. Bind off loosely.

Finishing

Pin center of sleeve top to shoulder seam. Sew sleeve to body, matching st for st. Join sleeve and side seams.

Carpentry

All wood sizes quoted in materials lists are actual, not nominal, (see 'Getting the Professional Look', pages 150–5)

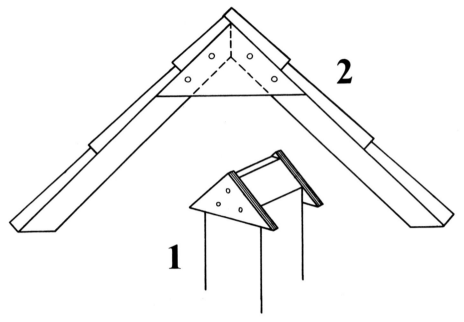

2

1

Hanging Bird Table

This project can be made largely from pieces of scrap lumber, and most of the measurements given may be regarded as approximate. The bird table does not need a high degree of finish; a certain roughness is part of its outdoor charm.

Materials
Roof Six 46cm [18in] lengths 10cm [4in] featheredge board
Base One 38 × 30cm [15 × 12in] piece 2cm [¾in] blockboard
Post One 40cm [16in] length 3.5cm [1⅜in] sq pine wood
Edge Strip Two 30cm [12in] and two 34cm [13in] lengths 3 × 1cm [1¼ × ⅜in] pine wood
Perches Two 18cm [7in] lengths 1cm [⅜in] dowel rod
Roof Supports Four 25cm [10in] battens 2.5 × 2cm [1 × ¾in]; 13cm [5in] square of 6mm [¼in] plywood
Other items One 3cm [1¼in] steel screw eye; 2.5cm [1in] galvanized nails; two 5cm [2in] No 8 flat head countersunk screws; 2cm [¾in] finishing nails (panel pins); wood glue; brown wood preservative

Cut a 90° wedge tip on the top of the post, then saw off the top 6mm [¼in], leaving a flat (diagram 1). Drill two 1cm [⅜in] holes through the post at right angles to each other, one 10cm [4in] and one 13cm [5in] from the bottom. Push the perches through, using a little glue, so that they project equally on either side. Make four

right-angled triangles of plywood by cutting the square twice diagonally and glue two of them to the post (diagram 1). Screw and glue the post to the center of the base.

Miter both ends of each piece of batten and make up two roof supports, pinning and gluing the battens together in pairs with the remaining plywood triangles (diagram 2).

Using galvanized nails, nail and glue the roof boards to the supports so that the supports are set in 5cm [2in] from the ends of the roof. Fix the boards from the bottom up, trimming off the top one on one side flush with the support, and the top one on the other side so it overlaps (diagram 2).

Cut or file a small flat midway along the roof ridge, then fix the roof to the post using glue and the screw eye. The screw eye is screwed through the flat on the roof ridge and into the top of the post. Pin and glue the shorter edge strips along short sides of base, then the longer ones on the longer sides so that they each overlap one end of the short pieces and leave gaps at diagonally opposed corners for brushing the table clean.

Finish with two coats of wood preservative.

Doll's Bed

A pine doll's bed is the kind of toy that is treasured long after its owner has outgrown dolls, and may well still be around to delight the next generation.

Materials

Headboard and footboard Pine wood board, 1×8.6cm [$\frac{3}{8} \times 3\frac{3}{8}$in]: two lengths 30.5cm [12in] (A); four 23cm [9in] (B) and two 15cm [6in] (C)

Bedposts Pine wood batten, 2×4.5cm [$\frac{3}{4} \times 1\frac{3}{4}$in]: four lengths 30.5cm [12in] (D) and four 23cm [9in] (E)

Frame Pine wood strip, 6mm $\times$ 4.5cm [$\frac{1}{4} \times 1\frac{3}{4}$in]: two lengths 38cm [15in] (F) and two 24.2cm [$9\frac{1}{2}$in] (G)

Bed knobs Four 3.8cm [$1\frac{1}{2}$in] wooden balls and four lengths of 1cm [$\frac{3}{8}$in] dowel 2.5cm [1in] long

Base One 3mm $\times$ 30 $\times$ 41cm [$\frac{1}{8} \times 12 \times 16$in] hardboard and scrap wood for base supports

Other items 2cm [$\frac{3}{4}$in] finishing nails (panel pins); wood glue; clear gloss varnish

For the headboard, take two long boards (A) and two medium boards (B). Ensure that the edges are true and level, then glue and clamp together with pieces A on the outside, and all pieces level at one end (diagram 1).

Similarly glue and clamp together two pieces B and two pieces C for the footboard.

When glue has dried, remove clamps and pin and glue the short pieces (G) of the frame to the headboard and footboard, level with middle pieces (B for headboard and C for footboard) and centered.

Glue two bedpost battens to one side of each board (D to headboard and E to footboard). The edges of the battens should fit level with footboard and headboard at the top, bottom and outer edges, leaving a 6mm [$\frac{1}{4}$in] gap between the short frame batten and bedpost for F. Cut away the waste wood (shaded area in diagram 1). The curved cut-out at the top of the headboard and footboard is 4cm [$1\frac{1}{2}$in] deep at the center. Glue the remaining battens to the other sides of the boards, thus completing the bedposts. Smooth the headboard and footboard with sandpaper.

Join headboard and footboard by pinning and gluing the two long sections (F) of the frame into place, level with the short pieces and the posts (see view from above, diagram 2). The nails are driven through into the inner sides of the posts.

Drill a 1cm [$\frac{3}{8}$in] hole in the four wooden balls 1.2cm [$\frac{1}{2}$in] deep and glue dowel in place. Use diagonal lines to find centers of the bedposts and drill 1.6cm [$\frac{5}{8}$in] holes to accommodate the dowels.

From the scrap wood cut eight small blocks (H) and glue them to the inside of the frame with their top surfaces 3mm [$\frac{1}{8}$in] below the frame's top edges (diagram 2). Cut the hardboard to fit the frame, then glue it into place on top of the blocks.

Sand the whole bed with fine sandpaper, then apply 2–3 coats of varnish.

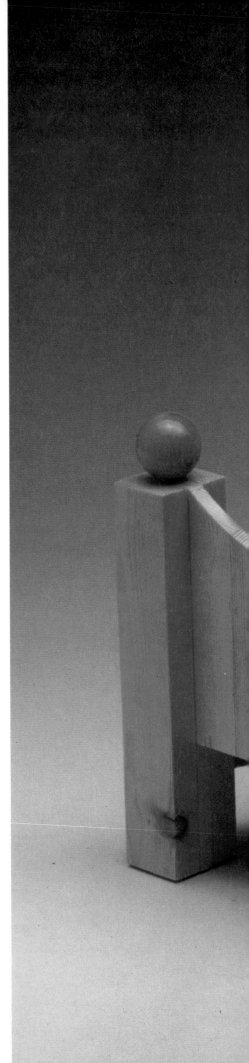

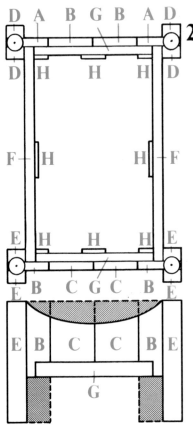

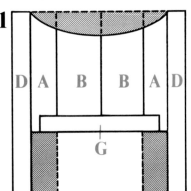

Plant Trough

The rugged charm of this plant trough, made from thick knotty pine, will not be spoiled if your cutting is a little inaccurate. It is designed to take three average-sized plant pots, (about 12cm [5in] diam. and 9cm [3½in] high) with a plastic tray underneath.

Materials
Pine wood Two pieces 2 × 20 × 26cm [¾ × 8 × 10¼in] for ends; one piece 2 × 14 × 50cm [¾ × 5½ × 20in] for base; two pieces 1 × 13.5 × 50cm [⅜ × 5¼ × 20in] for sides (we used joined lengths of tongue-and-groove paneling)
Quarter round molding Two pieces 1 × 12cm [⅜ × 4¾in]
Other items Wood glue; 1.5cm [⅝in] and 2.5cm [1in] finishing nails (panel pins); wood-filler; clear varnish
Note In diagram 1, one square = 5cm [2in]

Scale up the pattern for the end shape (diagram 1) on squared paper. Trace the shape on to each piece and cut out with a coping saw. Smooth off all cut edges with round or flat files or rasps as appropriate, then sandpaper whole piece smooth.

Place base and side sections together to make sure they are exactly the same length with perfectly squared ends. Rule a line on the base piece, 3mm [⅛in] from both long edges. Use the flat file or rasp to bevel the edges to this line (diagram 2). Sandpaper all three sections smooth.

To assemble first center one of the lengths of quarter round molding horizontally to the inside base of each shaped end section so that the top flat edge is 3.5cm [1⅜in] from the base of the shape; glue and pin in place. On the inside of each side section draw a line 3cm [1¼in] from the bottom to mark the position of the top edge of the base. Glue and pin sides to base along these lines; drive finishing nail (pin) heads below surface. Glue and pin end sections in position, with base sitting firmly on the quarter round molding.

When glue has dried fill pin holes with wood-filler, sand down and finish with 2–3 coats of varnish.

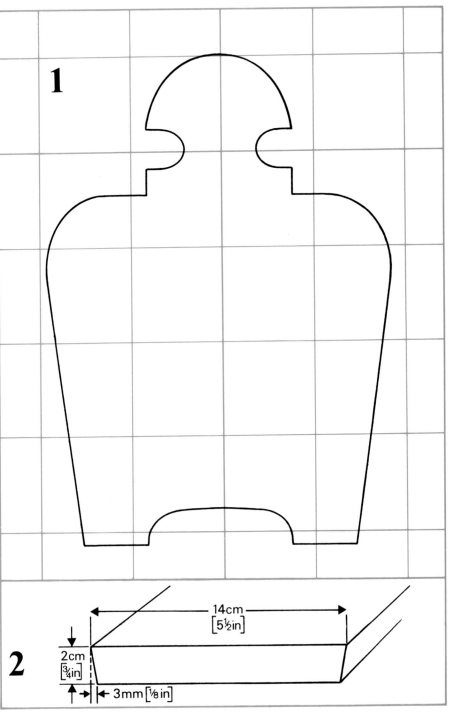

Pull-Along Train

This sturdy little green locomotive and freight car make an ideal present for a 2- to 5-year-old. If you have the time and patience you could make it even more fun by adding extra cars.

Materials

For locomotive
Plywood or blockboard One piece 12mm × 35 × 35cm [½ × 13¾ × 13¾in] for base, cab, coal car and wheels
Pine wood One piece 2.5 × 2.5 × 45cm [1 × 1 × 17¾in] for axles; one piece 10 × 6 × 13cm [4 × 2½ × 5¼in] for boiler
Dowel rod One 2.5 × 12cm [1 × 4¾in] for smoke stack and pressure dome
Other items Wood glue and epoxy resin adhesive; six 3cm [1¼in] No. 8 screws; six 4cm [1½in] mirror screws and six washers; green and red paint; two small staples; 1m [1yd] cord; one toggle

For car
Plywood or blockboard 12mm × 26 × 20cm [½ × 10¼ × 8in] for base, sides, ends, wheels
Pine wood One piece 2.5 × 2.5 × 30cm [1 × 1 × 11¾in] long for axles
Other items Four 3cm [1¼in] No. 8 screws; four 4cm [1½in] mirror screws and four washers; one small cup hook; wood glue; epoxy resin adhesive; paint as for locomotive.

Size

Locomotive 35cm [13¾in] long × 17cm [6¾in] high
Car 20cm [8in] long × 10cm [4in] high

Locomotive

Cut out plywood parts as follows:
Base (A) 35 × 14cm [13¾ × 5½in]
Cab roof (B) 13 × 11cm [5⅛ × 4⅜in]
Cab front (C) 11 × 9.5cm [4⅜ × 3¾in]
Cab (D) and *coal car (E)* sides (see diagram 2)
Cut from one piece 12cm wide × 9.5cm high [4¾ × 3¾in], placed as in diagram 2 so curved cut is shared. Coal car is 8cm [3⅛in] high
Coal car back (F) 8.5 × 8cm [3⅜ × 3⅛in]
Wheels (G) Six 6cm [2⅜in] diam

To assemble, either pin and glue or dowel and glue the pieces together. Work in the following order (diagram 1).

Drill 2.5cm [1in] holes in cab front, 1cm [⅜in] from top and 1.5cm [⅝in] from sides; and in cab sides, 1.5cm [⅝in] from top and 1cm [⅜in] from sides. Round off corners of cab roof, cutting around a coin, and bevel all around with a file. Fit these pieces together. Paint, except base edges and front.

Smooth top edges of coal car; fit pieces together and paint, except base edges.

Round off top edges of boiler (H) as for cab roof; also corners of base. Glue boiler centrally on base, 3cm [1¼in] from front edge. Glue cab to base and back of boiler. Glue coal car to base 3cm [1¼in] from back edge.

Drill two 2.5cm [1in] holes in boiler for smoke stack and pressure dome, in center, 3.5cm [1⅜in] apart, to a depth of 2.5cm [1in]. Cut smoke stack (J) and and pressure dome (K) from the dowel rod, 7.5 and 4.5cm [3 and 1¾in] high respectively. Shape top of pressure dome with coarse sandpaper. Glue in place and paint remainder of locomotive (not under base).

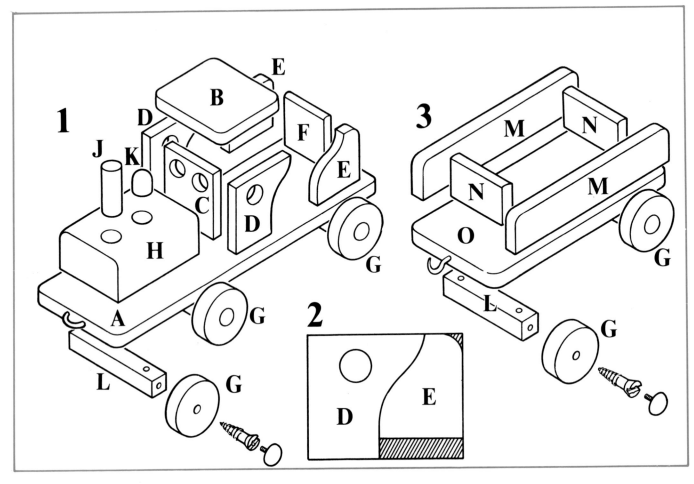

Cut axle wood into three equal pieces. Glue and screw axles (L) under base, first one 5cm [2in] from front edge. Leave a 5cm [2in] gap; fix second axle; leave a 14cm [5½in] gap and fix third axle. Use two No. 8 screws in each. Paint base, axles and wheels.

Drill a hole through wheels and assemble on axles with mirror screws, placing washer between wheel and axle, and gluing the caps on with epoxy resin glue to fix them permanently. Do not tighten the screws too much, or the wheels will not turn. Fix staples to front and back of base, tie cord through front one and put other end through toggle.

Trim with red paint as shown in photo.

Car
Cut out plywood parts as follows:
Base (O) 20 × 14cm [8 × 5½in]
Sides (M) 16 × 5cm [6¼ × 2in]
Ends (N) 8.5 × 5cm [3⅜ × 2in]

Assemble as for locomotive (diagram 3). Screw cup hook to one end and decorate as for locomotive.

Book Rest

Here's a present with many uses: for reading at the table; supporting cook books or magazines; or for holding notes at an easy-to-read angle when typing. If you can't do curved sawing, just saw off the top corners and gently round off the line with a coarse file. See photograph on pages 74 and 75.

Materials

Birch plywood One piece 6mm × 27.5 × 25cm [¼ × 10¾ × 10in]; one piece 6mm × 20 × 7.5cm [¼ × 8 × 3in]; two pieces 6mm × 7.5 × 1.2cm [¼ × 3 × ½in].
Quarter round molding One piece 2 × 25cm [¾ × 10in]
Other items 5cm [2in] brass hinge with screws; two small screw eyes; three 1.2cm [½in] No. 6 flat head countersunk screws; one metal-tipped cord fastener; wood glue; clear gloss varnish; enamel paints for decoration
Note In diagrams, one square = 2.5cm [1in]

Scale up the pattern for the shaped top (diagram 1) on graph paper. Use carbon paper to trace it on to one of the shorter sides of the larger piece of plywood and saw with a coping saw or power jig saw. Saw back rest or prop (diagram 2) out of the smaller piece of plywood, using half of the profile for the top shape.

Sandpaper all the wood pieces to a fine finish. Screw and glue molding flush with lower edge of book rest. Glue one piece of wood strip flush with top edge of prop; the other with its top edge 20cm [8in] up from the bottom center back of rest. When dry, screw the hinge to the strips.

Apply 2–3 coats of varnish. Decorate the top as desired – we used a motif from the selection on pages 144–9. Finally place screw eyes centrally in prop and back of book rest, 10cm [4in] up, and join with the metal-tipped cord fastener.

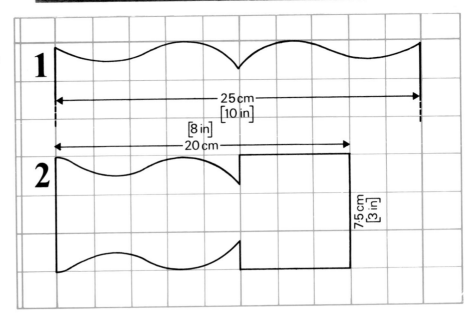

Pegball Game

This game is a 3D version of noughts and crosses (tic tac toe): two players each aim to get a complete row of their color pegballs in any direction on the board. Tiny tots also enjoy playing with it just as a fun toy, moving the pegs around from hole to hole. See photograph on page 103.

Materials
Pine wood One piece $2.5 \times 20 \times 20$cm [$1 \times 8 \times 8$in] (or join three pieces as we have done)
Wooden balls Ten 4cm [$1\frac{1}{2}$in] diam.
Dowel rod 2×35cm [$\frac{3}{4} \times 14$in]
Other items Wood stain in two contrasting bright colours; wood glue; clear gloss varnish; 20×20cm [8×8in] square of felt

Mark drilling points on the piece of pine as in the diagram. Drill 2cm [$\frac{3}{4}$in] diam. holes at these points to a depth of 2cm [$\frac{3}{4}$in] (wrap masking tape around the drill as a depth gauge).
Drill a 2cm [$\frac{3}{4}$in] hole in each ball to a depth of 1.2cm [$\frac{1}{2}$in]. Cut ten 3cm [$1\frac{1}{4}$in] lengths of dowel rod and glue them into the balls.

Sandpaper all components to a fine finish. Stain five pegballs in one color and five in the other.

Give the pegboard and balls 2–3 coats of varnish, but leave the dowels and insides of holes unvarnished. Glue the square of felt to the bottom.

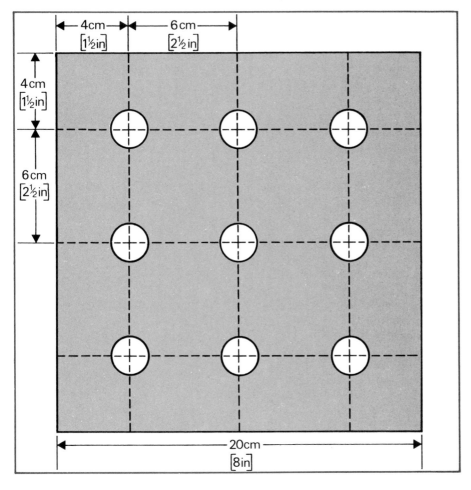

Wooden Spoon Box

A simple pine box to hold kitchen spoons is not too difficult for a youngster to make for mother; all that's needed is the ability to saw the pieces of wood nice and square so they will fit together. We've added a personal touch – her sign of the zodiac, from the set on page 147. Also see photograph on page 48.

Materials
Pine wood 1.5 × 12 × 75cm [$\frac{5}{8}$ × 4$\frac{3}{4}$ × 30in]
Other items Twelve 3cm [1$\frac{1}{8}$in] finishing nails (panel pins); wood glue; wood-filler; clear gloss varnish; small quantity of enamel paint for motif

From the wood, cut one 25cm [10in] length for the back; two 12cm [4$\frac{3}{4}$in] lengths for the base and front and two 7.5cm [3in] lengths for the sides. Saw two corners off the back piece with a sloping cut from points 4cm [1$\frac{1}{2}$in] each way. At the same end, drill a 6mm [$\frac{1}{4}$in] hole in the center, 4cm [1$\frac{1}{2}$in] down.

Bevel or chamfer one edge of one 12cm [4$\frac{3}{4}$in] piece (base) to a width of 1.2cm [$\frac{1}{2}$in].

Sand all pieces to a smooth finish with fine sandpaper, at the same time slightly rounding the 'shoulders' at the back. Pin and glue the sides to the back, level at bottom and with end-grains butting on to the back. Then pin and glue on front. Finally pin and glue base to box, flush on three sides and with chamfered edge projecting at front. A couple of finishing nails (panel pins) in each joint should be enough.

Drive all the finishing nail (pin)

heads below the surface and fill holes with wood-filler (also fill any slight inaccuracies in the joints). Smooth down with fine sandpaper and finish with two coats of varnish.

Motif
Scale up your chosen motif on graph paper so that it measures about 10cm [4in] square over all (see directions on page 155). Use carbon paper to transfer the motif to the front of the box.

Paint as desired; if more than one color is used, let the first one dry before adding another.

Spice Rack and Jars

Designed to hold six small spice jars, this is a present which you can adapt to suit the person it's for. We've made the rack complete with jars and spices, but you could just as well give it on its own, with a set of gold labels, with commercial spice jars (adjust size of rack to fit if necessary), or with empty jars and labels. See photograph on page 48.

Materials
Pine wood One piece 1 × 5.5 × 122cm [$\frac{3}{8}$ × 2$\frac{1}{8}$ × 48in]
Brass screws (with cups) Fourteen 2cm [$\frac{3}{4}$in] No. 4 flat head countersunk
Other items Wood glue; finishing nails (panel pins); wood-filler; clear varnish
For spice jars
Jars Six empty mustard or other suitable jars
Enamel paint
Other items Self-adhesive labels; six pieces of wire; six spare lids

Cut the wood into two 24.5cm [9$\frac{5}{8}$in] lengths and four 16.5 [6$\frac{1}{2}$in] lengths. In one of the short pieces drill a 2.5cm [1in] hole halfway along and as close as possible to one edge. Make straight cuts from the hole to points at each end, 1.1cm [$\frac{7}{16}$in] up from the opposite edge (see diagram). This forms the broken pediment top. Sand all pieces to a smooth finish with sandpaper.

Mark and drill six holes for screws in each of the two long pieces (sides) at points 1.5, 11.5 and 21.5cm [$\frac{5}{8}$, 4$\frac{5}{8}$ and 8$\frac{1}{2}$in] from the top end and 1.2cm [$\frac{1}{2}$in] in from each edge. If rack is to hang up, drill two similar holes in the pediment, 2.5cm [2in] from ends and 1.5cm [$\frac{5}{8}$in] from bottom edge.

Lightly pierce ends of shelves correspondingly to locate screw points, then assemble, applying glue to shelf ends before screwing tight.

Glue pediment along rear edge of top shelf, and then fix with a finishing nail (panel pin) at each end. Drive heads below surface and fill with wood-filler.

Finish with 2–3 coats of varnish.

Jars
Thoroughly wash and dry the jars. Cut circles out of the self-adhesive labels about 2.5cm [1in] diam. and stick on for 'windows'. For a perfectly smooth finish, dip each jar into a can of paint up to its neck – hang by a wire hooked through a hole drilled in a spare lid. Leave hanging over newspaper to drip dry. Remove labels and paint lids as desired.

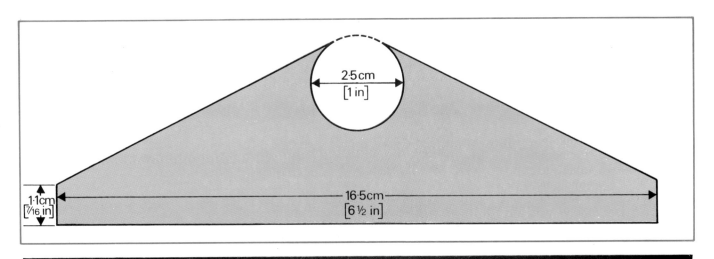

2·5 cm
[1 in]

16·5cm
[6 ½ in]

1·1cm
[7/16 in]

Corner Shelf Unit

An old-style shelf unit is just the thing to give teenagers to hold the multitude of treasures they always collect in their rooms. It would look equally at home in a kitchen or in a living room, displaying china and glass. See photograph on pages 74 and 75.

Materials

Pine wood Two pieces $2 \times 22 \times 100$cm [$\frac{3}{4} \times 8\frac{5}{8} \times 39$in]; one piece $2 \times 15 \times 100$cm [$\frac{3}{4} \times 5\frac{7}{8} \times 39$in]
Quarter round molding One piece 2×100cm [$\frac{3}{4} \times 39$in]
Other items Sixteen 3cm [$1\frac{1}{4}$in] No. 4 flat head countersunk screws; wood glue; masking tape; 2cm [$\frac{3}{4}$in] finishing nails (panel pins); four 4cm [$1\frac{1}{2}$in] No. 8 flat head countersunk screws with eyelets; varnish
Note In diagram 1, one square = 2.5cm [1in]

Place the best-looking sides of the two large pieces of pine wood together and bind around at intervals with masking tape, ensuring edges are level right down the length. Use try-square and saw to cut one end of this 'sandwich' perfectly square. Measure 20cm [8in] from the sawn-off end and rule a line across the wood; use the try-square to continue the line around the 'sandwich'. Measure and mark a line 2cm [$\frac{3}{4}$in] beyond this in the same way. This marks the position of the first shelf. Measure and mark three more shelves in the same way, allowing 16cm [$6\frac{1}{4}$in] between each one and 2cm [$\frac{3}{4}$in] for the thickness. Measure 20cm [8in] beyond the final shelf position and saw the wood off square.

Scale up the shape (diagram 1) on graph paper. Cut out and transfer to each end of the 'sandwich', marking on each side of both ends. Using both panel saw and coping saw, cut through both pieces of wood together (to ensure shape matches on both sides of unit). File and sandpaper the sawn edges smooth. Remove tape and separate the pieces. Mark lines for shelf positions lightly on the inside of the wood with the try-square.

Make a cardboard template to cut four shelves from the remaining pine wood (diagram 2). The angle at a is a right angle; a–b equals width of wood. On the shaped pieces drill two holes for screws 6cm [$2\frac{1}{2}$in] from the ends in each marked shelf position; countersink from the back. Glue one short side of each triangular shelf and place in position on the inside of one shaped section. Secure with two No. 4 screws. Repeat with second shaped section. Glue and pin quarter round molding into the angle between the two shaped sections at the back. This forms a rounded corner to help the unit fit into an unsquare wall corner.

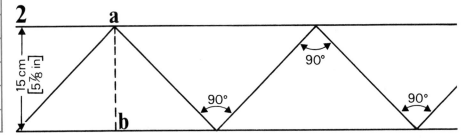

132

Marquetry

This beautifully patterned little box for storing jewelry or other small treasures is a good present for the experienced craftsman to make. If you lack the skill to make a perfect box you can start with a bought one about the same size and adapt the marquetry pattern to fit. The really ambitious can take the project a step further by fitting a musical movement inside to play a tune when the lid is raised. See photograph on page 80.

Materials

One box made of 1.2cm [½in] plywood, 15cm wide × 11.2cm deep × 8.7cm high [5⅞ × 4⅜ × 3⅜in] – flat, hinged lid 1.2cm [½in] deep
Veneer A pack of assorted marquetry veneers
Brass fittings Pair 2.5cm [1in] hinges with screws; small clasp (with pins)
Other items Contact adhesive; clear matt varnish; craft knife

The patterns given are actual size to fit the box dimensions above. (If you design your own pattern keep to similar simple shapes.) They show how we alternated the colors and grains of the veneers, and set them off with 3mm [⅛in] cross lines of rosewood.

Transfer the design on to the lid (diagram 2) and sides of the box (diagram 1); pencil it in accurately and adjust the size if necessary. Make sure cross lines on lid match up with those on sides. Use the side pattern for back and front, enlarging the center pieces. Tape tracing paper over the box and copy the design; this tracing is used to mark the veneer. Sort out the veneers you have and plan which wood to use for each section of the design, making sure that there is enough of any given one to complete the job, and remembering that you will need some to line the inside. If you are using a bought box, remove hinges and clasp before applying veneer.

Before starting to cut the veneer, coat all sides and lid of the box with contact adhesive and let dry. Put carbon paper under the tracing and copy each shape on to the chosen veneer. Cut out with a steel ruler and a *very* sharp craft knife. Hold ruler down

tightly but only apply light strokes with the knife, or the veneer will tear. Also try to cut *into* a sheet of veneer rather than out to the edge, to avoid splitting. Change the knife blade as you work to ensure that it is always razor sharp.

Start with the lid, in center of design, and work outwards, gluing each piece with contact adhesive, brushed thinly on and allowed to dry, before cutting the next. When you reach an edge, leave a tiny overlap of veneer so that the marquetry on the other side will form a flush corner.

When all pieces are in place carefully smooth down with fine sandpaper. Veneer the insides and smooth down, making sure the edges are nicely rounded so that the joining of veneers is nearly invisible. (If the job is well done the finished box will look almost as if made of solid hardwoods.)

Fix the hinges, cutting away the veneer so they are recessed, and pin the clasp to the front and lid lip.

Finish with 2–3 coats of clear matt varnish.

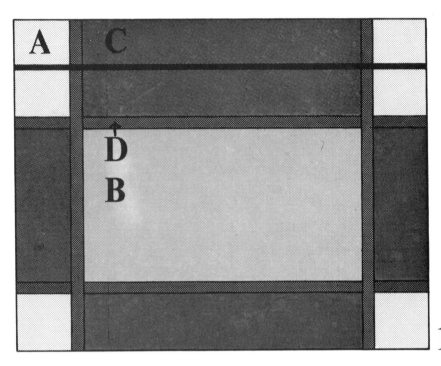

A – walnut
B – beech
C – mahogany
D – rosewood

1

2

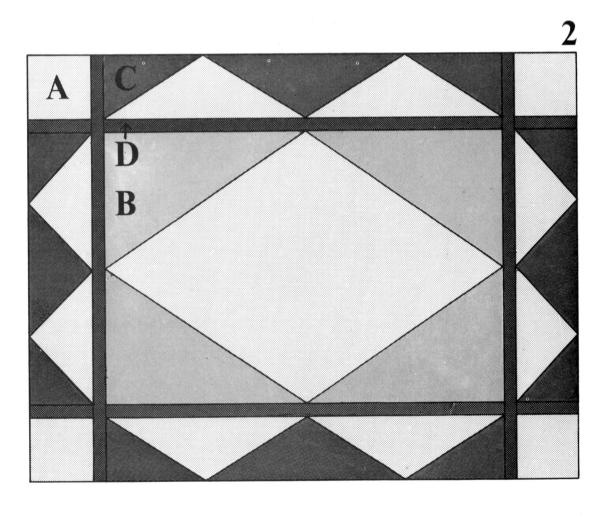

135

Child's Stilts

Stilts are traditional toys that still hold great appeal for children. The ones shown here are for a child of 6–7, so the steps are not far from the ground, but you can easily adapt them for an older child: use sturdier wood, make stilts longer and steps higher. See photograph on pages 74 and 75.

Materials

Pine wood Two pieces 2 × 4.5 × 102cm [¾ × 1¾ × 40in] for uprights; two pieces 2 × 11 × 15cm [¾ × 4½ × 6in] for steps
Wood screws Six 7.5cm [3in] flat head tenpenny (No. 10 countersunk) screws.
Other items Wood glue; wood-filler; rubber pieces; nails; clear gloss varnish
Note In diagram 1, one square = 2.5cm [1in]

Shape the step pieces with a coping saw or powered jig saw so that one side is curved (diagram 1), and the bottom is 4cm [1½in] wide. (If you don't have tools for curved cutting just saw a straight slope as shown in diagram 2, leaving the bottom 4cm [1½in] wide.) Place the steps against the narrow side of the uprights and mark their position: top of step 30cm [12in] up from bottom of upright.

Round off or plane all edges of uprights except on the area that meets the back of the step. Sandpaper all four pieces thoroughly to avoid any danger of splinters.

For maximum strength position the screws as in diagram 1. Drill holes for the screws through the upright, with the first 1cm [⅜in] slightly wider than the screw head to allow for counter-sinking the screw. Glue and screw steps to the uprights and fill holes with wood-filler. Finish with sandpaper and 2–3 coats of varnish.

To prevent slipping attach a piece of rubber to the bottom of each stilt with nails.

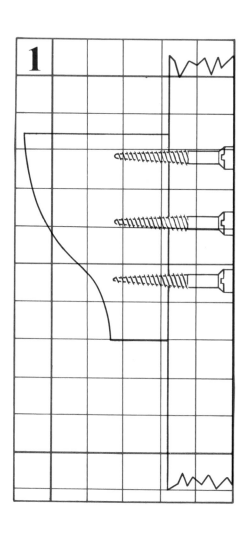

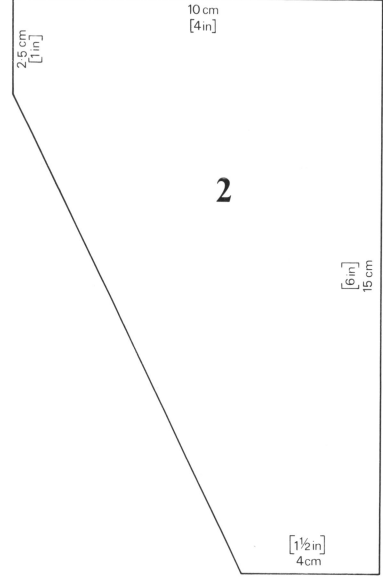

Wine Rack

Although it looks so professional, this 'mahogany' wine rack is not hard to make, but it does depend on accurate marking, cutting and drilling so that the pieces fit together precisely to form six perfect squares to take six wine bottles. See photograph on page 26.

Materials

Hardwood strip 6 × 2.5mm × 530cm [¼ × 1in × 17ft] to be cut in lengths as directed below

Dowel rod 2 × 100cm [¾ × 36in]

Brass screws (and cups) Twenty-four 2.5cm [1in] No. 6 flat head countersunk

Other items Wood glue; red mahogany wood stain; clear gloss varnish

Cut the hardwood strip as follows: four 45.5cm [17¼in] lengths; eight 33cm [12½in] lengths; four 20.5cm [7¾in] lengths.

Cut the dowel into twelve 7cm [2¾in] lengths.

Drill holes for screws down the center of each wood strip as follows:

All strips 4cm [1½in] from each end.

Long strips Also drill 16.5cm [6¼in] from each end.

Medium strips Also drill one halfway.

Pierce each end of the dowels at center with a bradawl to receive screws. Bring all pieces to a good finish with

138

fine sandpaper and give them two coats of stain.

When dry, assemble as shown in the picture. The screws pass through intersections and into the dowel ends.

Before attaching the final strip dab wood glue between the intersecting pieces, then tighten up, checking that the bottle spaces are correctly square.

Finish with two coats of varnish.

Presenting Your Presents

The way that you wrap up the gift you have made is almost as important as the item itself. A lumpy brown paper package just doesn't arouse the same excitement and anticipation as something neatly wrapped in brightly colored paper and decorated with pretty things. Wrapping can serve a practical purpose, too, in disguising the shape of instantly recognizable gifts like records or bottles, and, when items have to be sent by mail, in ensuring that they reach their destination safely.

Almost any gift makes a greater impact if presented in a box, so save all the commercial containers you possibly can: paper tissue cartons, cheese boxes, plastic cartons and trays, empty chocolate boxes, shoe boxes – anything that comes your way. Or you can make your own from cardboard, following the instructions in this chapter. Little fancy cartons like the one with handles on it are surprisingly easy to make, and make a gift look really special, even more so if you use gold or silver cardboard. They are particularly good filled with candies; as are the enchanting woven heart baskets.

Cookies and cakes, because of their oil content, need careful wrapping. Either use plastic or cellophane bags, or if putting in a box, line with greaseproof or waxed paper. For candies, individual paper wrappers are ideal, as they protect each one and lend a very expensive look. Plastic-wrap is also useful, not only in protecting the item but also in enhancing its appearance.

Although it's well worth spending a lot of time and effort on presenting your presents, there's no need to spend a fortune on materials. This chapter shows how, with a little imagination, you can create attractive wrappings using simple materials. Choose your wrapping papers according to the size of the presents, saving expensive metallic foils for small ones, and using inexpensive paper with some kind of decoration for big ones. And never waste any – surprisingly tiny scraps can be used to wrap small items once you know how to do it; and even tinier pieces can be cut up and added on as appliqué decoration.

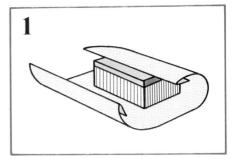

See photograph on title page; and for Woven Heart Basket on page 23.

WRAPPING PRESENTS

When wrapping presents don't use too much paper – this gives a bulky, messy result as well as being wasteful. The picture sequence shows the correct method, whether you are using decorative paper, or brown wrapping paper for a package to be mailed.

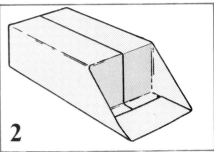

1 Cut paper large enough to cover all sides of the package plus about 2.5cm [1in] all around. Place package in center. Fold in two ends of paper and bring to top, one end overlapping the other. Seal folded edge with tape.

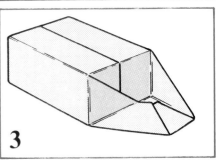

2 Tuck in the other two ends by first pushing down each center piece (which should be slightly longer than height of package). Straighten out the flaps on either side.

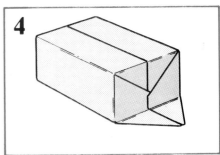

3 Fold the outer flaps into the center, and flatten the lower ones. Overlap one lower flap over the other and tuck in the end to make a point; this makes a triangle.

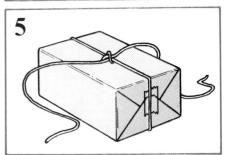

4 Bring the triangular flap to the center of the package and secure with tape. For a gift package finish with colored tape and decorations as desired.

5 For a brown paper package going by mail finish by tying with string. Bring string around to top and secure with a slip knot. Turn over and knot on the other side tightly; trim ends.

6 Stick on a clearly addressed label to the recipient. Also write on your own name and address so that if the package should go astray it won't end up in the dead letter office.

SOFT ROUND PACKAGE

Crêpe paper is a good choice for soft or awkwardly shaped presents as it can be stretched.

Materials

Crêpe paper; rubber band; double-sided tape; rosettes

Place the present on a large square of crêpe paper. Gather the paper around it and secure with a rubber band, leaving a paper ruffle at the top. Trim this neatly and arrange evenly. Make rosettes as shown below and arrange around top of package with double-sided tape.

ROSETTES

Rosettes like these can be made in any size and color to suit your present.

Materials

Gummed gift tape (sticky gift ribbon) in yellow, orange and green; scraps of crêpe paper

Cut the gift ribbon into 25cm [10in] lengths as follows: two orange, two yellow, four green. Back orange and yellow lengths to each other, and green to green. Twist the orange and yellow lengths into figure-eights. Repeat with green lengths.

Gather a small square of crêpe paper to form the center as shown in the diagram and stitch. Sew this to the orange/yellow ribbons, and these to the green ribbons. The ribbons should be stitched to one another at right angles. At the base sew on 2–3 crêpe paper leaves.

Make up as many rosettes as desired and place on the parcel.

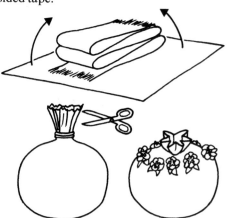

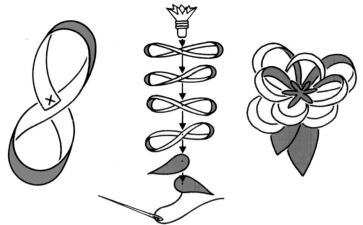

CYLINDRICAL PACKAGE

Tube-shaped wrapping is a good disguise for a present which can be rolled, such as a sweater. A black and gold color scheme gives a very exclusive look.

Materials

Cardboard tube; black and gold striped paper; black tape; shiny gold tape

Roll paper around the tube and join the seam with black tape. Fold in the ends in the same way as for a rectangular package, although it cannot be as neat. Seal with tape. To cover the ends, make curls from colored tape: back black and gold tape to each other and curl over scissors. Stick in place.

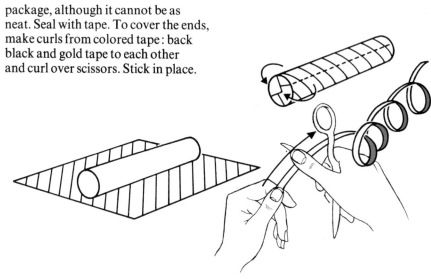

PYRAMID PACKAGE

This shape makes a real mystery gift – it's impossible to guess what's inside.

Materials

Cardboard; wrapping paper to cover; clear tape

From the cardboard cut four equilateral triangles measuring 40cm [16in] each side. Cover one surface of each triangle with wrapping paper, folding over at edges and sticking to the back. Use clear tape to join A–A, B–B and so on, leaving E–E and F–F until the present is inside.

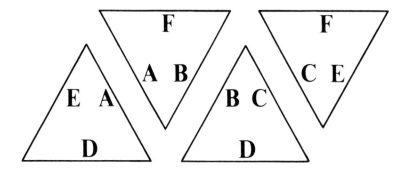

MYSTERY OWL

The wise owl can conceal either a record or a large book under his feathers.

Materials

Two sheets contrasting wrapping paper in muted tones; thick cardboard; brown and white tape; double-sided tape; paper paste

Cover present in wrapping paper. From cardboard, cut out the shape of an owl's head and shoulders, following the diagram. Also cut two wings. Cover all these in the same wrapping paper. For the feet, cut two rectangular pieces of cardboard as shown; score and bend in half widthwise. Cover with contrasting paper.

For face, cut out eyes and beak from multiple widths of white tape; stick on. Also cut and stick white face feathers. Add brown and white pupils. Make a feathery breast with a patch of the contrasting paper, cut zigzag around the edge; paste on.

Secure head and wings firmly to body with brown tape. Glue feet to base as shown, so that they will support owl upright.

WOVEN HEART BASKET

Although they look so delicate woven heart baskets made of gift ribbon are actually very durable, and can be used many times over to hold candies or tiny presents. Hang them on the Christmas tree, or give them to children as little extra presents.

Materials

Two rolls adhesive gift ribbon (colored sticky tape), in contrasting colors

From each roll cut five strips 18cm [7in] long. Back each strip with the same color. Lay the five of one color side by side. Across each end set three rows of the same color to sandwich the band and hold it in position. Shape as in diagram 1 and fold in half. Repeat with second color tape and weave the two together as in diagrams 2, 3 and 4.

Open out the heart-shaped basket and stick a 22cm [8½in] long, backed strip inside to hang it up.

TREASURE CHEST

Here's an economical way of gift-wrapping a really large package

Materials

Large carton (from supermarket); brown paper to cover; thin cardboard; gold shiny tape; black cloth tape; double-sided tape

Wrap carton containing present neatly in brown paper, following the basic method described for wrapping packages. Draw wood-grain marks over the surface with brown crayon. Bind the edges in gold tape and stick two cloth tape straps around as shown in picture.

Make strap buckles from squares of cardboard covered with gold tape, and lock and key-hole from cardboard covered with gold and cloth tape. Stick on trunk with double-sided tape. Cut handles from cardboard; cover with gold tape, and attach to each end.

BLUE BOX WITH ROSE

Designed for a small, select gift, this package is wrapped in metallic paper which reflects the delicate, near-transparent rose.

Materials

Clear tape; green tissue paper; map pin; florists' wire; metallic paper.

Stick multiple widths of clear tape back to back. From these, shape little rose petals with scissors, cutting about seven the same size. Cut a length of wire to form the stem; wrap tightly in green tissue, and bind firmly with clear tape. To assemble the rose, place the petals evenly all around one end of the stem with small tabs of clear tape (see diagram). Gently curl back petals with scissors. Use pin for center.

Leaves Cover one side of a strip of green tissue with clear tape and shape into a rose leaf. Stick on to the stem with a tab of clear tape, uncovered side upwards.

Wrap gift in metallic paper; curl the stem and stick in place.

In diagram, a – curls and b – tab of tape.

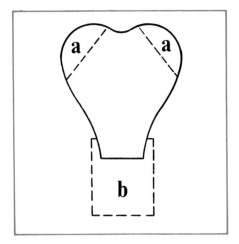

MAKING CARDBOARD CARTONS

These are quite simple to make by the method for a square carton shown here. The sides of the carton are joined with clear tape. If the carton is to be covered with wrapping paper afterwards you don't have to be too neat about this. But if it is made of colored cardboard there are three possibilities: use clear tape long-hinge-fashion on the outside so it hardly shows; use the tape *inside* (dfficult not impossible); or use contrasting tape and make it part of the design.

The cartons can be made to any size you need: calculate what size the base should be, then for a cube-shaped carton make all the other squares the same. The bigger the carton the thicker the cardboard needs to be. The diagrams show the simplest type of carton – a cube – but the principle can easily be adapted to make rectangular boxes. As long as base and top are identical, and the four sides are of equal height, it will work.

Square Carton

Cut out cardboard (diagram 1). Score along the broken lines, and fold inwards. Using tape, fix the edge of A to B, B to C, C to D and D to A. Square E becomes the base of the box and F the lid.

Carton with Window

Diagram 2 shows the lid of the carton. Cut this out of cardboard as shown. Score along the broken lines and fold inwards. To make the window, cut a hole inside E as shown. Glue a piece of cellophane or plastic across the hole on the inside. Using tape, join edge of A to B, B to C, C to D and D to A.

For the base, cut cardboard in the same way, but fractionally smaller, so the lid fits snugly over. Omit the window.

Carton with Handles

Cut out cardboard (diagram 3). Score along the broken lines and fold all inwards except those at G. Fold those two outwards. Using tape join A to B, B to C, C to D and D to A. Square E is the base. Cut a slit in the lid, F, as shown, and slot the handles through.

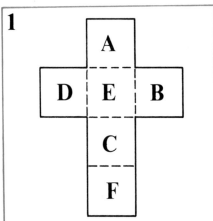

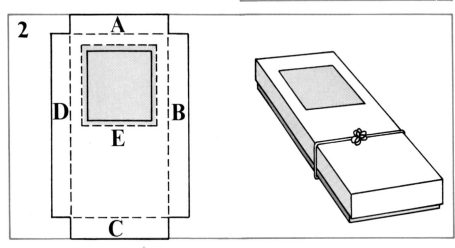

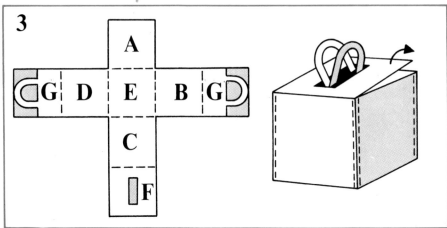

- - - - fold line

143

Motifs

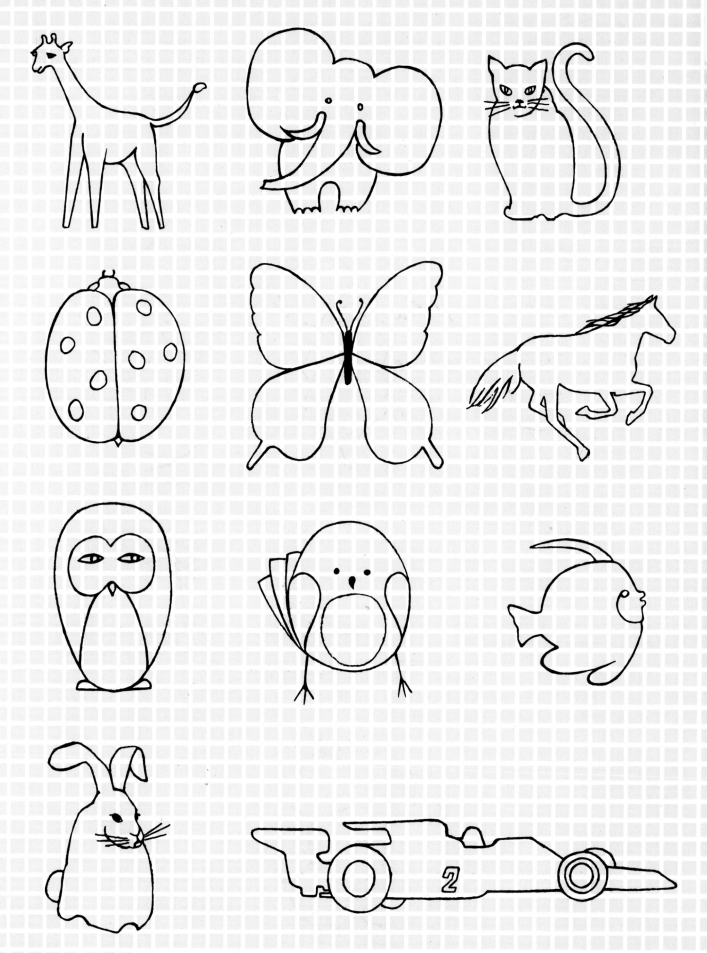

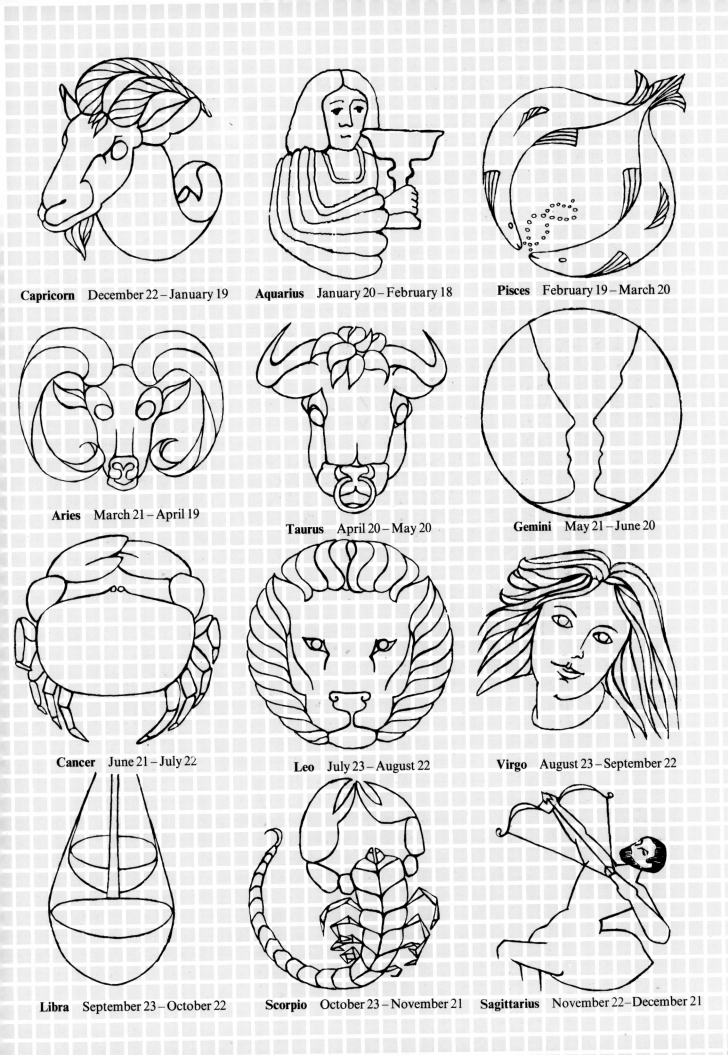

Capricorn December 22 – January 19

Aquarius January 20 – February 18

Pisces February 19 – March 20

Aries March 21 – April 19

Taurus April 20 – May 20

Gemini May 21 – June 20

Cancer June 21 – July 22

Leo July 23 – August 22

Virgo August 23 – September 22

Libra September 23 – October 22

Scorpio October 23 – November 21

Sagittarius November 22 – December 21

ABCDEF
GHIJKL
MNOPQ
RSTUV
WXYZ

abcdefgh
ijklmnop
qrstuvw
xyz 123
4567890

Getting the Professional Look

If something you make is not a success, or causes endless trouble to get right, very often the reason is lack of knowledge of some basic techniques. In this section you will find hints and tips to help you avoid problems, whether in knitting or crochet, craft work, cooking, carpentry or sewing. If you are already experienced in the technique in question you probably won't need them; they are mainly intended for people trying new techniques for the first time, or perhaps with only a little experience.

Obviously the tips cannot be comprehensive, but we have tried to cover basic points which can make all the difference between success and failure; between something which looks amateurish and something which has the mark of a professional.

Metric and Imperial Measurements

Throughout this book measurements have been given in both the metric system and the more familiar linear, liquid and dry measures. Please note that you must *never* mix the systems.

Knitting and Crochet

Crafts

The golden rule for success in both knitting and crochet is: *check the gauge or tension of your work before you start*. This is particularly important with the patterns in this book, because no brand names of yarns are used, and the one you buy may very well not knit in exactly the same way as the one we have used.

So although it may seem tedious to work the number of rows given, and persevere until you achieve the right size on that number of rows, it's well worth making the effort. Only by doing this can you be sure the garment will come out the size you want.

Most of the patterns in this book use basic stitches, with which you will be familiar, but where something more elaborate is called for, it is well worth doing a test piece. In this way you will not only find out if you are making any mistakes, but will familiarize yourself with the technique, and when you come to make the actual garment, the work will be easier and quicker.

When you have completed the knitting or crochet work, don't spoil it by careless finishing. Regard your work as an *haute couture* article and take pains to finish it correctly.

The best way to sew the seams is to match the row ends together and slip-stitch loosely with the yarn used for the garment (split strands if too thick). Do not pull the stitches up tightly or the seam will pucker.

The conventional way to make sure the pieces are the right size and shape is to lay them out on an ironing board, wrong side up, and put pins all the way around the edges, checking the measurements with a tape measure. The pieces are then pressed lightly before sewing together. However you may find you achieve better results by sewing first, then placing the garment around an ironing board (not on the flat) and coaxing it into the shape required by gentle pressing.

Whichever method you use, make sure to press as instructed on the yarn label. Different types require entirely different treatment, ranging from a hot steam press to a cool dry one. And never iron ribbing – this reduces its elasticity.

Many a beautifully knitted or crocheted garment has been ruined by careless washing. Synthetic yarns can stand fairly rough treatment, but those with a high or all-wool content should always be washed by hand in lukewarm water, in soap flakes or mild detergent, and never rubbed, just gently squeezed. Rinse well, squeeze gently to remove water, then lay out on a towel and arrange in the correct shape. Roll up and leave for several hours before taking out to dry, preferably with it lying flat. After this treatment pressing should hardly be necessary; if it is, use a cool iron lightly.

Many different craft techniques are used in this chapter so there isn't room to give instructions for all of them. However there are certain ground rules that generally apply.

If you have never tried a particular craft before, don't plunge in and expect to produce immediately something as good as that shown in the picture. Experiment and practise first. You are bound to have failures, but don't be discouraged; it is only from failure that you will learn how to succeed.

Equip yourself with the right tools. Very often these are no more than pencils, scissors, a craft knife – nothing you can't get in the local stores – but they must all be sharp. Materials often called for are tracing paper, graph paper and carbon paper which can be found at any art, craft or general variety store.

We have not included any crafts where expensive tools or equipment are needed, but a few, such as macramé, do call for some special but inexpensive items, and these can be obtained from the suppliers of the materials (see page 6 for a list of mail order firms to use if you have no local craft shop).

Before starting work, read the instructions through carefully to make sure you understand them and that you've got all the necessary tools and materials. Think about what you're going to do before you do it, and don't rush – work slowly and carefully, concentrating on every step. Don't think too much about getting your project finished; enjoy the work for itself.

Although a lot of the charm of craft work lies in its slight irregularities as compared with smoothly finished, machine-made, mass-produced articles, this doesn't mean things are

Crafts

sloppily made. Be as precise as you can in measuring and cutting, so that something supposed to be right-angled truly is, and a square is a square and not a diamond. When sewing, there's nothing wrong with large stitches – but unless you're doing free-form work like the embroidered owls, they must be evenly spaced and straight, not all over the place.

And here's a special tip for children: make sure your hands are clean! Grubby fingermarks do not improve the appearance of any craft work.

For work involving painting in different colors, make sure one is dry before starting on the next, otherwise the two will run together and ruin the job.

With enamel paints it is very important to keep dust at bay, and that includes dust, hairs and bits of fluff coming from you, your clothes and family pets, also dust in the brush itself. When varnishing, make sure you have the right type for the paint you have used, for example, some types of varnish cannot be applied over gold or silver paint. For craft work the most suitable paints are enamels sold in tiny containers; or you can just as well use remnants of enamel paint left over from decorating.

Another area where correct choice is important is in glues: the wrong one can be disastrous; for example, a special adhesive is a must for sticking styrofoam (polystyrene) balls, as other types cause them to dissolve. In general, clear glue, sold under many brand names and usually in small tubes, is suitable for most craft work. Paste, which can be spread over a larger area faster, is good for large-scale paperwork; rubber-based adhesive is good for fabrics and felt, and rubs cleanly off the fingers. Where a really strong bond is needed, for hard surfaces like metal or shells, choose a 2-part epoxy resin adhesive. (The new super glues must be handled with great care, as they are so quick-acting and strong they have been known to weld people's fingers together! Not for use by children.)

Finally a word on design. Very often craft work that doesn't look too good when finished has suffered from over-elaboration. There is a temptation to keep adding finishing touches, ending up with something fussy. It's much better to keep shapes simple, colors restrained. That doesn't mean you can't use bright colors – but don't put too many different ones together, and choose them with care. Keep an eye out for balancing colors if you don't want your work to look either too bright or too drab.

Cookery

The recipes chosen for this book have deliberately been kept simple so that anyone may try them. But nevertheless, just as in craft work it pays to practise.

Cookies are practically foolproof, as long as the dough has been refrigerated so that it doesn't stick to the worktop (if it does get sticky just put it back in the refrigerator for a while.) But it's worth baking a few before putting the whole batch in; oven times and temperatures given can only be approximate, as unfortunately individual ovens can actually be hotter or cooler than their indicators show.

If you have never baked before, make an ordinary fruit cake before embarking on a rich, expensive one. And make some plain bread to learn how yeast behaves and how to handle it, before you try your hand at a Stollen.

For making candies and marmalade there's no doubt that a sugar thermometer is a great help, dispensing with a lot of worry and guesswork. But here again, practice makes perfect. If you don't have a thermometer your first batch of candies may not be good enough to give away, but the children will enjoy them. And if your marmalade doesn't set, it can always be boiled again.

When making pâté make sure that the fat topping forms a perfect seal to the meat; it will not keep if there is an air hole.

Whatever you are cooking, be ultra-fussy about kitchen hygiene. Have everything spotless, chase out the family pets and make sure children wash their hands before they become involved.

Finally pay particular attention to packing and wrapping. Food that is not nicely presented can often look unappetizing.

152

Sewing

Unless otherwise stated, all the patterns include a 1.5cm [⅝in] seam allowance.

The yardages given are based on the width of the fabric we actually used. Naturally, what you buy may well be in a different width, so check this when buying. In most cases your fabric is likely to be wider than ours, so you would need slightly less of it. We have been fairly generous with the yardages, as there is nothing worse than running out of fabric in mid-stream. So if you want to economize, cut out the paper pattern pieces first and lay them experimentally on a given width to find out exactly how much fabric to buy.

All the items included in this book can be sewn on an ordinary domestic sewing machine. A zigzag or automatic needle will speed up the work as you can use the zigzag stitch to finish raw seam edges. Zigzag stitch is also used for appliqué work; small items like motifs can be done by hand, but for large items like the appliqué quilts a zigzag machine is essential.

Check that the needle in your machine is sharp – if you have been sewing nylon at any time it has quite likely become blunted, and a new, sharp one will make the work go much more easily. An average needle is suitable for all the things we have made, except those in canvas. To sew this, buy a heavy-duty needle – an ordinary one may not go through several thicknesses of this heavy fabric, and even if it does it will almost certainly break before you finish.

Our instructions are written on the assumption that you have some experience in dressmaking. For those who haven't, here are a few tips.

Enlarging diagram patterns is a somewhat slow process, but not difficult to get right if you work carefully. Buy some dressmaker's graph pattern paper and copy the shape of each pattern piece shown to the scale indicated, working in pencil so you can make corrections. Each small square in the book will be a bigger one on your paper. Before cutting out the paper patterns, check carefully that the overall shape is right – that you haven't included an extra line of squares by mistake – and that curved lines are faithful copies of the original. Copy any directions like 'cut 2' or 'fold'. (Keep the paper patterns after cutting the fabric in case you want to make the item again.)

Pin the paper patterns to the fabric and check before cutting out that you have the right number, and that any sides marked 'fold' are actually on one. The patterns should run straight up and down the grain of the fabric, not at odd angles.

Assemble the pieces in the order given, always pinning and basting before you machine stitch. (Basting means sewing together temporarily with big stitches.) It's a good idea to press seams open as you go, while they are easy to get at.

Raw edges that will remain exposed should be finished by running a zigzag stitch down the edge; failing this, oversew by hand or clip with pinking shears. (Do zigzag before sewing, hand finishing afterwards.)

On seams that are turned to the inside – as on a pillow or cushion cover or any bag construction – the seam allowance should be trimmed to about 6mm [¼in]. At a corner, don't follow around at a right-angle, but cut across diagonally, as close to the stitching as possible. The corner will then be nice and square when turned out, not lumpy or bulky. On a curved seam, make a few snips into the seam allowance to help it ease when turned out.

Finished items should not be washed, as this removes the crisp brand-new look; just give them a light final pressing.

Carpentry

While we hope that some of the projects will attract experienced woodworkers, nearly all of them are fairly simple and can be successfully attempted by newcomers to the craft (to whom the following tips are mainly addressed).

There are no difficult joints, and careful and accurate work counts for more than experience. For any one project only a few basic tools are needed, and the following equipment is sufficient to make everything:

Steel tape rule (never use a dressmaker's tape measure: it stretches)
Try-square for ensuring square marking
Panel saw for general cutting
Backsaw (tenon saw) for finer cutting
Coping saw for cutting curves (or a power jig saw for speed)
Miter box as a cutting guide
Hammer
Screwdriver
Replaceable-blade craft knife
Handbrace or power drill with drill bits and counter sink (it can also be useful to have a ratchet brace and auger bits)
Bradawl
Flat-faced nailset (nail punch)
Sanding block and sandpaper (medium and fine grades)
Vise for holding work (a portable one can be clamped to a table)
Pair of clamps (10cm [4in] size)
Flat and round wood files or rasps
2.5 and 1cm [1 and $\frac{1}{2}$in] paint brushes

Buying Wood

Softwoods like pine are sold by their 'nominal' sizes, which are slightly larger than their actual ones. This is because the wood is classified by size before it is planed at the lumber mill. Generally the difference between the nominal and the actual size is about 3mm [$\frac{1}{8}$in] each way, though even this can be a little more or less.

For these reasons wood sizes given here are the actual sizes we used, and if you cannot find wood exactly of the size specified you can make allowances for this when working if you read the instructions carefully beforehand and study the illustrations so that you understand the designs. Always take a steel tape rule along with you to the lumber yard. In a stack of boards some will usually be closer to the size you want, and might even be exactly right.

Make sure the wood you pick is not bowed or warped. The best way to do this is to sight along all of the edges. The foreshortened view easily shows up any bends that shouldn't be there.

Accuracy

'Measure once, cut twice; measure twice, cut once' is an old carpenter's saying well worth heeding. Your steel tape rule should be in constant use.

So should your try-square. For wooden components to fit together they must be cut 'square'. If a cutting line is marked with a try-square and the cutting is done carefully you should get an accurate right-angled cut, but the 90° slot of a miter box will help to ensure this.

Cutting

Let the saw do the work – that is, don't bear down heavily on it. A good sharp saw needs little more than its own weight in use and sawing 'light and easy' gives far more accurate cutting. Pressure tends to make the saw swerve.

When cutting plywood it's best to mark your cutting lines on both sides of the wood (not difficult if you're careful), then score both sets of lines with a sharp knife before sawing. This ensures that the underside veneer does not splinter. Always cut with the good side up.

Don't saw right down the cutting line: it will give you an under-size component. Cut on the 'waste' side of the line with the saw skimming the line.

When starting to saw across a board get the cut going first with a few *backward* strokes of the saw to avoid splintering the edge.

Gluing

Wood adhesives have improved in recent years, and if you follow the manufacturers' instructions they enable you to make sturdy wood structures with the minimum of nails and screws. But a glued joint must have some pressure while setting. Small components may be held in a vise while they set, or placed on a table with weights on top. Others need more care. For instance, if you wish to glue boards together edge-to-edge you have to set up a 'cramp'. A good way is to lay the boards on a flat surface between another board that is clamped to the table and still another one that is against the projecting rods of a partly open vise. When the vise is closed the components will be pressed together. Not much pressure is needed but it must be firm and steady.

'Pin and glue' is a common instruction. It means that you use finishing nails (panel pins) as well as glue. Very often the nails are merely to hold the piece in place while the glue sets. In such a case you lightly punch the almost headless pins a little below the wood surface and fill the holes with wood-filler.

Always wipe away the surplus glue that is squeezed out of joints under pressure while it is still wet, using a damp cloth.

Motifs

Sanding

To give the best finish use medium sandpaper first, then fine. Thorough sanding is essential if clear varnish is to be used to best effect.

Most people know you have to sand 'with the grain', that is, on the flat sides and long edges of the wood you sand to and fro along the *direction* of the grain, never *across* it. The trade secret is what to do with the end grains. These you can sand to and fro for hours without result. The reason is that they must be sanded in *one direction only*. To find out which way rub a finger along the grain; it will feel slightly less rough in one direction than another, the smoother one is the sanding direction. Rub the sandpaper that way, then lift it off and do it again; never rub the opposite way. End grains can be very beautiful when treated in this fashion.

An exception to this is when the end grain is on a curved cut. It's still one-way sanding, but following the curve from the shortest boards to the longest. For example, the curves in the head and footboards of our doll's bed have to be sanded from the center outwards, each half separately.

Finishing

For finishing we have mostly used clear gloss varnish as it is easy to use, gives a good finish and wears well. For a really professional gloss 2–3 coats should be applied, rubbing down the surface lightly with very fine sandpaper or steel wool before the final coat.

When using varnishes, paints or stains, follow the manufacturers' directions. They know best.

The selection of designs and motifs on pages 144–9 is intended for you to copy and use to decorate your gifts, or to give a present a personal touch like the recipient's initials or sign of the zodiac.

If the motif is not the right size for your purpose it is quite a simple matter to enlarge or reduce it. To enlarge, draw a grid of small squares over the motif – 6mm [¼in] is a convenient size. (Trace the motif on to tracing paper if you don't want to draw in the book.) On a sheet of plain paper draw out a grid of *exactly the same number* of squares, but larger by the amount you want to enlarge the design. So if the original motif measures 5cm [2in] high and you want it to be 10cm [4in], you would draw a grid of 1.2cm [½in] squares – twice as big as the original.

Conversely, to make a motif smaller, draw a grid of large squares over it, and transfer to a grid of smaller ones.

To transfer the design from the paper to the article to be decorated, put carbon paper underneath and go over the lines of the design with a sharp pencil. If you have no carbon paper, shade over the back of the paper with a soft pencil and then go over the design with a sharp pencil. Because this produces a much fainter line, it doesn't work too well on a soft surface like fabric.

The designs and motifs can be used in many ways: painted on to wood or other hard surfaces; appliquéd on to fabric; cross-stitched on to canvas; embroidered on to knitting; painted on to fabric with fabric dyes, or drawn on with fabric crayon; cut out of cardboard in reverse form and used for stenciling; machine- or hand-embroidered.

Choose your design carefully according to the technique you are going to use to reproduce it. Obviously if you are painting you have the greatest freedom, and a fancy shape is no problem. But for appliqué work or stenciling, simple large shapes, such as the teddy bear and apple we have used in the sewing chapter, are best.

For embroidering on to knitting, or doing cross-stitch, choose a simple design and transfer it on to graph paper. The tiny squares then represent stitches on knitting, or squares on canvas. Block out the design to the nearest square, then lightly crayon in the colors to be used. Work in blocks of color – you cannot do fine lines or details.

The alphabet is easiest to reproduce in paint or crayon. If using appliqué, practise first on scraps of fabric and make the letters as large as possible. For examples of lettering, both painted and appliquéd, see the sewing chapter, pages 58–85.

Index